FORTY-ONE PAGES

ᗪᐣᏏᑎ

OSKANA POETRY & POETICS

John Steffler

Forty-One Pages

On Poetry, Language,
and Wilderness

University of Regina Press

Printed and bound in Canada at Friesens. The text of this book is printed on 100% post-consumer recycled paper with earth-friendly vegetable-based inks.

The glyph on the cover and those throughout the text of *Forty-One Pages* are drawings of signs from the El Castillo cave in Spain, reproduced by Duncan Noel Campbell. They represent early written symbols and also, therefore, a kind of page, the beginning of the long tradition to which this book is dedicated.

Cover and text design: Duncan Noel Campbell, University of Regina Press

Proofreader: Donna Grant

The text and titling faces are Arno, designed by Robert Slimbach.

Canada Council   Conseil des arts
for the Arts   du Canada

Canadä

creative
SASKATCHEWAN

Library and Archives Canada Cataloguing in Publication

Title: Forty-one pages : on poetry, language, and wilderness / John Steffler.

Names: Steffler, John, 1947- author.

Series: Oskana poetry & poetics.

Description: Series statement: Oskana poetry and poetics | Poems.

Identifiers: Canadiana (print) 20189067985 | Canadiana (ebook) 20189067993 | ISBN 9780889775879 (softcover) | ISBN 9780889775886 (PDF) | ISBN 9780889775893 (HTML)

Classification: LCC PS8587.T346 F67 2019 | DDC C811/.54—dc23

10 9 8 7 6 5 4 3 2 1

UNIVERSITY OF REGINA PRESS
University of Regina
Regina, Saskatchewan
Canada S4S 0A2
TELEPHONE: (306) 585-4758
FAX: (306) 585-4699
WEB: www.uofrpress.ca
EMAIL: uofrpress@uregina.ca

We acknowledge the support of the Canada Council for the Arts for our publishing program. We acknowledge the financial support of the Government of Canada. / Nous reconnaissons l'appui financier du gouvernement du Canada. This publication was made possible with support from Creative Saskatchewan's Creative Industries Production Grant Program.

for Susan Gillis & Phil Hall

CONTENTS

I

Corner Window

In the early half-light I usually make tea and sit surrounded by books near the windows in the southwest corner of the room. Like a photographic print developing in a chemical bath, Woodshed Hill's outlines slowly emerge behind the west-facing glass; the south window to my left gradually fills at this time of year with a snow-covered field. For the past few weeks the eyes I've opened each morning have been partly Cézanne's: I open Götz Adriani's catalogue of Cézanne's paintings where I've left a bookmark and turn the page: plate seventy-one, "Large Pine and Red Earth." The world-material spell. Stillness in things.

Before I have stepped out of the house, even before the outdoor world is discernable in the windows, I will have passed through a series of pages under the reading light and will likely have opened my notebook and filled a few pages with observations and fabrications of my own. These pages will be passageways to the rest of the day—perhaps programs, themes the extent of whose influence has no clear end. Being steeped in the page, being so accustomed to its landscape and creatures, it is hard to say where the natural world begins and what in the surrounding, oncoming world does not belong to a page.

What are some of the books scattered around my chair? *Cézanne Paintings*, Margaret Atwood, Robert Macfarlane, Anton Chekhov, Knud Rasmussen, Javier Marías, Clarence Glacken, Emily Dickinson, *Salt and Silver*, Nikolai Leskov, Samuel Beckett, *On the Art of Fixing a Shadow*, Thoreau, Xi Chuan, Susan Howe, Michel de Montaigne, *Chagall and Music*, Walter Benjamin, Christine Desdemaines-Hugon, Jean Clottes, Bashō, Peter Wohlleben, Max Oelschlaeger, Hans Peter Duerr, Jorie Graham, Tomas Tranströmer, John Kinsella, Daniel Everett, Louise Glück. Below this layer are others I can't see.

There are many kinds of page. What signs and expressions will appear there? What world or mind will they seem to be coming from and what will they hatch in your mind? Will you welcome what the page conveys, will it fade quickly or leave a lingering pleasure or distaste? Will the page in some way change you forever?

And if you prepare to make marks on a page, what will you put there? What will you send by way of the page for someone to receive?

Signs of various sorts cluster on the page. Its customs and messages relate to occasions of waiting, receiving, discovering and offering. The potentiality of the page, the expectancy it sets up is related in my mind to the archetypal events of birth, hatching, sprouting and other sudden arrivals: a new life, a new presence might appear there to share our personal world and engage our energies. Versions of the ancient experiences of hunting and fishing are embedded there: the attentive waiting and observation, the sense that at a distance some encounter is pending, something will be met with and captured. Stargazing, watching for danger, watching for a lover, watching for seasonal signs, for ripening plants, approaching weather. The page can be experienced as an offering of food, as offering or receiving a gift.

Yes, yes, the page is a clay tablet marked with an inventory of wine jars, but before that it was a clearing where something might appear, where the movement of time, the world's changing narrative was epitomized. The page is a performance space. It is an area framed by expectation and practiced conjecture: a ritual space, a forum for appearances and disappearances.

And when we write? We speak to someone or something absent. We detach our words, our intentions, from ourselves and send them out or leave them to be found. We hunt inside ourselves, watch for a birth in language on an inner page and give a performance in words.

It seems to me that what is at the heart of literature, what is most meaningful in it, involves a speaking to someone or something absent or distant. This involves a faith in space and time and perhaps a belief in fate or destiny: that the message (the information, the thought, the wish) that has been sent or left will travel or wait unchanged, intact, and meet with its intended recipient at some future time. This is clearly at work in a letter or a prayer but also in every poem, story and song, every diary entry and tombstone inscription. There is no need to leave messages for those who are immediately present. In the remote past I imagine our preverbal ancestors would have communicated with those nearby using gestures, touches, glances and vocal sounds, but once they began devising and leaving signs for those not present—markings, selected objects, shaped objects, images—they were already engaged in a kind of writing. I think of that ancient sign-making as lying just under the surface of what I'm doing here.

So, the page is still a clearing in time and space, a kind of axis point where we might have contact with those elsewhere and in another time. On its periphery are the dead, the gods, our past and future selves as well as everyone we might want to contact for whatever reason. The signs we send through the page and that appear there have the power to cross barriers of time and space and dimensions of being. They can pass from one heart into another like travelling dreams. Clearly, signs sent like this—with metaphysical force—are the language of spirits and a means to communicate with the powers that move the visible world.

If we go into a cave (some form of cave) and wait for signs to appear to us and scratch those signs on the cave wall, we are at the doorway between the spirit within us and the spirits in the surrounding world. I think the page is always a version, a descendant, of this place and action: a passageway where a spirit coalesces, defines itself, and goes to meet other spirits—perhaps to win their favour, perhaps simply in fellowship or to strengthen their company. In any case, the page is much older than paper or clay tablets.

And the modern blank paper page, although it looks empty, is an architecture of rules, a court awaiting some statement, some display of meaning. It is a room in which no one is welcome who cannot trade in symbols, who cannot recognize themselves in mirrors or recognize the outlined shapes of conifers, stars, elephants, mice. The cat, for example, sees nothing meaningful in the mirror or in the mouse I am drawing for him right now. He wants to sprawl across this page in the hope that I'll stop scratching the paper with my pen and instead scratch him behind the ears.

For book lovers the page is, first, always a welcoming home where the writer can get to work and the reader can journey and make discoveries in a state of great privilege; but there are gaps and discontinuities on the page for both reader and writer. This is partly because the reader is also a kind of writer and the writer a kind of reader.

The reader cannot be merely a passive recipient of the words on the page. The act of reading is a collaboration in which the reader reconstitutes the information—the ideas, the emotions—condensed and encoded in the text, although the reader rarely reconstitutes everything the writer has sent out without some critical reservations. For some readers the writer's offering is a kind of found material to be taken up and fashioned into a new structure. But for most readers the art of reading—perhaps the pleasure in reading—is partly the art of suspending disbelief. In the same way, in the theatre the audience members' imaginations work with what is onstage and lit up; they welcome the unknown nature of what's behind the scenes and unseen in the dark margins. On both the page and stage what we can't see, what we can't anticipate, is as important as what we can see and predict.

In choosing a clearing in which to witness things arriving, we are also choosing the obscure surroundings from which they arrive. As readers, we participate in creating the written event, but that participation goes only so far. Ultimately, we want the signals to come from somewhere off the page, offstage, outside the book. We want a gift, a thing that augments us: the world opening before us. This is a compensation for being ignorant mortals. An all-seeing god can never be lost or separate from an environment, can see everything coming and therefore can never be surprised or discover anything new. But, as limited mortals, we set out on a fairy-tale journey over and over. Opening a page highlights that moment.

And for the writer—for the poet especially—this whole process has its internal, subjective analogue. I, at least, find this is true of much of my own experience as a writer. What I write is not purely a creation of the page. It does not start and end entirely on the page's built environment. It's possibly a delusion for me to think that what I'm putting on paper has some more remote origin than the conventions of language and the page themselves, but this is a delusion I need to keep—a gap in attention and control, a region behind the scenes and offstage that frames and, in a sense, supplies the lit clearing where the words get set down.

What is gratifying—what is *necessary*—in writing and reading is the sense that some experience, some discovery has occurred off the page, on the margin of culture if not entirely outside it, in the not-yet-known region of nature, in the world we don't fully control. What this involves, I suppose, is a reliance on intuition, a process in which the writer's imagination is itself a kind of stage upon which things appear. The act of writing, the craft, is in large part a preparation of the page, a theatre-building. We make a clearing and watch with all the learned skill of our culturally structured tradition to see what will walk out of the unknown surroundings into the open space.

Using words, we try to make the reader's page resemble this space.

My idea in writing these pages is to explore my own lifelong relationship with language and writing, but I find myself generalizing that relationship and speaking of "our" use of language and the way our immersion in words affects our subjective experience and our interaction with the natural world. Why do I do this? Am I imitating linguists and philosophers who theorize about the role of language in human culture and behaviour? Do I hope to join the ranks of Jakobson, Saussure and Chomsky? Hardly. I'm a poet with an interest in the relationship between the human-created world we occupy and the raw, natural world we also occupy in often problematic, sometimes graceful, sometimes unacknowledged, unexplored ways.

I think one of the reasons I generalize my experience of language is that I don't assume that relationship is unique to me. I'm sure I use English in slightly idiosyncratic ways, that I have a style or voice of my own, but I also have no doubt that I speak and write fundamentally the same way as countless other people. A shared vocabulary and syntax has to be the basis for linguistic communication. And I have inherited language along with a culture and a biological history. Although the particularities of my life are personally mine, I think of the language I've inherited—an accumulation of thousands of years of ancestral experience from a vast range of eras, places and situations—as something like a sea I swim in or the land I was born in. My experience of language is in many ways transpersonal. And yet it's the personal living-in-language that interests me as well as language's broad role in culture.

I like to believe that I can think of language generically, as a human custom or practice, and that it's possible to imagine or know the world beyond language. Perhaps I'm deluding myself. Perhaps I am so much the product of my specific language that I can never experience or imagine anything that is free of its matrix. I do have the sense, though, that the natural world is itself inherently nameless—an integrated whole, a continuous anatomy—to which people have applied language like a transparent film imprinted with a map, diagrams, outlines demarcating certain features and processes. I think of this template of naming being applied not only to the natural environment but also to our sensory and emotional experiences and to our dreams. I think we can (here I am using "we" again) experience the external and internal worlds in ways that go beyond language and then try to bring those experiences back to be framed and shared in language. The tools, the implements of language both enable and formalize that process.

Why do I make this kind of pronouncement? I'm exploring my experience of writing and language in an effort to discover points of influence, points of energy, insights that can initiate further engagement and making. I am looking for insights into what I take to be a real, factual world; I am not hunting for gratifying fantasies; but nor am I trying to arrive at settled conclusions. In fact, each time I set out to explore my experience I tend to take slightly different routes and arrive at different discoveries—hence the ongoing writing, the accumulation of pages. The discoveries might overlie each other or sit at odd discordant angles or contradict each other. I accept that. All that matters to me is that what I'm discovering seems honest and true, a depiction of a real experience.

I'm not interested in promulgating an unassailable theory. I recognize that you might not agree with things I've said so far about writing and language; your experience might be different or, even if it's similar to mine, you might not be as confident as I am that it is common to all. What I hope, however, is that, instead of simply pushing my ideas away and going on with something else, you get some pleasure, some energy from exploring your own experiences of these things. This is what I look for in essays. I read not to have my prejudices and settled opinions confirmed but for prompts, for sparks of ideas that stimulate my imagination, my memory, my appetite for making things and investigating the world. This is what is still so exciting about Montaigne's essays. His rather pedantic scholarship is of his time, but his honest inquiring imagination is entirely modern and timeless. That's more what I'm trying to imitate.

It's possible, I imagine, that the names of things might not seem like arbitrary human impositions on the world but rather like channels, arteries reaching out from things or creatures to people, channels whereby energy and spirit flow from one to the other. Perhaps it is my English or Indo-European heritage and the industrial culture to which I belong that has caused me to seek experience beyond the reach and template of language. But I think it would be too easy for me to blame English. I notice that Lao Tzu in the sixth century BCE wrote (or was quoted as saying), "The way that can be spoken of / Is not the constant way...The nameless was the beginning of heaven and earth." This is how the *Tao Te Ching* begins. Translations vary, but the idea is clear: reality cannot be directly represented or apprehended in language. Zen and other spiritual practices have also recommended wordless silence or have deliberately confounded the conventions of language and logic to achieve a direct experience of reality.

So, I use the universal "we" when I think of the broad human use of language, but I wish to apologize if this seems blindly arrogant or presumptuous. English—this increasingly global, international language, one of the key languages bound up with industrial culture—is my first language. If my or my parents' first language were an Indigenous language or that of a cultural minority—perhaps a language threatened with extinction—I imagine the word "language" and the phrase "our use of language," at least at first sight, would mean something quite different to me.

Here's my linguistic biography. I grew up speaking English but with German, in the form of Pennsylvania Dutch, as a peripheral, vestigial language in our home. My paternal ancestors had come from German-speaking Alsace in the early nineteenth century; my mother's grandparents had come from northern Germany in the mid-nineteenth century. Both their families had lived for generations in the Kitchener-Waterloo area in Ontario and had continued speaking German as their first language up to my parents' generation. When my mother or father came out with a German word or expression, it was usually in a joking way that would lead to memories of how things used to be when they were growing up, memories of relatives or old customs or events. In this way I learned a smattering of disconnected German words and sayings that enabled me to surprise and amuse German-speaking people I met later in life. I could say: "Greif zu!" or "Greif es!" ("Dig in!" or "Grab it!") at the start of a meal and make everyone laugh.

My consciousness of a German background meant that I always felt a bit like an outsider. Most of my friends came from immigrant families, and I did not identify with the British-Canadian mainstream.

I studied French through five years of high school and on into the first years of university where I read French literature and wrote essays in French. I studied Latin from grades ten to thirteen in high school and had some of my strongest early experiences of poetry while translating poems by Virgil and Catullus. I studied Japanese for half a year in grad school in Toronto and had a Mombusho scholarship to study in Japan, but my life changed direction at that point and I went instead to Newfoundland, which offered its own linguistic and cultural education. I've learned a few words of Greek and Spanish along the way. Learning French and a little bit of Japanese (which I've now forgotten) showed me that different languages bring with them different ways of feeling, knowing and being in the world.

While I recognize that it's always going to be contentious to speak of "our use of language" as a broad human practice because there are so many different languages and so many ideas about language, there is another human collective—another "we"—that I think it's important to acknowledge. This is the "we" that refers to our current industrial-technological culture. I think it's important to recognize our participation in this increasingly global collective even when we resist it in the name of preserving a different way of life. For, even when we resist it, even *as* we resist it, its influence on each of us individually and on the planet as a whole remains profound and is increasingly destructive. There is a paradox in this because this global culture is in some ways deeply attractive; it offers unparalleled general wealth and security—or seems to—at the same time that it is wiping out local traditional cultures, causing widespread species extinction and endangering human survival. Perhaps dissociation around this issue, the paralysis some of us experience in dealing with it, has something to do with being accustomed to living inside a language-based cultural bubble, at a distance from the natural world, assuming we will always inevitably figure out a technological solution to our practical physical problems. I say "our problems" because I think most of us now belong to this industrial-technological culture. Membership is not determined by the language we speak or our conscious affiliation (although some people—for example, Donald Trump—do actively extol this culture); it is defined not by ethnicity or religion or race but simply by our participation in a material economy, a material way of life. If we make use of mechanized transportation, especially fossil fuel–based, metal industry–based transportation such as cars, trucks, buses, trains, airplanes and ships, or if we make use of any products this kind of transportation provides—non-local food, refrigerated food, clothes we don't sew, cloth we don't weave—we belong to the industrial-technological culture. It includes everyone who depends on electronic communication and information, the electricity grid, the pharmaceutical and medical industries, and any mass-manufactured and retailed commodities. I clearly belong to this culture even though I don't identify with it. I've benefited from it (without timely medical care I would not be alive now), but I regret what it's doing and where it's headed.

It's interesting to try to work this out: we are only partly—perhaps only marginally—autonomous individuals. We are caught up in an economy, in a social network, in a culture. This is also a linguistic issue: we are caught up in a language. How can we come to terms with the collectives to which we belong? How can we influence them to change their direction? How can we change or free ourselves in their midst?

Laying down row after row of words, one after another—especially typing them—is a kind of miniature masonry. The page, walled up with print, is a bit like the Church Militant, like those square-faced cathedrals in the style of a fortress, asserting with stolid belligerence the convictions of their congregations. A shared language already displays what its speakers generally think about things—how they name and organize the world—but to feel the need to write these things down suggests an anxiety about change, a distrust of the future, a dislike of contradiction, a frailty of self-image, and in sum a desire to establish authority.

Or the page is the opposite of this: a Trojan horse that looks like a grim cathedral, but when you open the doors out rush comedians, poets, vandals, mice.

Is the page always a guide to some place? A map—or an effort to recall a map—to help return there?

Half reconstruction, half conjecture: indoors, on the map table, in the diary, we try to recall what happened to us out there, what we heard and saw; we try to sort out a sequence, warning signs, associated phenomena, so that when we're out there again we might be better prepared to make sense of what's going on.

Or have a good alibi for being out there. An argument that's stronger than any evidence.

Why did I write about the Grey Islands? Why didn't I just go there and keep quiet about it?

I invented the Grey Islands on the page. A memory of a feeling of encountering something too large and wild to be held. The page was the sea-crossing, the ordeal, the danger, the unknown, the discoveries, the learning, the days added one to one, the lonely vigil.

Walking around, camera in hand, hunting for photos is a good way to slow down and become more deeply aware of one's surroundings—up to a point. The camera, and with it the aim of looking for significant images, can stimulate an interest in colours, textures, compositions, the dynamics of light and motion, the working of time, the signs of causation and consequence. In its unselective objectivity the camera can confront us with signs of pain and good fortune, ruin and renewal, and trouble our brittle standards of beauty, safety and decency. But while the camera justifies and encourages looking, it also limits it. The camera requires a kind of looking suited to its technology, its range and abilities. It can go only so close, it can take only so much in, its focus and its response to light and shadow are crude and mechanical, it is confined to surfaces. The camera sees indiscriminately and factually, it sees more than we are in the habit of seeing as we hurry through the world thinking of other things, but it always sees according to its built-in principles as a machine.

And what's more, as we take the camera out hunting for photos, we inevitably engage in a tradition. We have a visual language in mind, a sense of what makes a good photograph, what makes a 'picture,' an interesting image. Even if we set out to contradict or avoid all the conventions of painting, photography and visual symbolism that we're aware of, we are still caught up in the dynamics of an inherited language. And this language involves breaking down the totality and wholeness of our integrated sensory experience and, further, breaking down and channelling our visual experience in terms of practical technique. It involves selecting, limiting, framing or shooting randomly, focussing or blurring, but inevitably freezing something at some point in its constant becoming, turning it into something it is not, into an image, an object unconnected to what it was and to whatever it has become since the photo was taken.

In this sense, broad, unmediated looking—watching—is nothing like using a camera.

There are some parallels between photography and writing, the camera and language. Long ago we became human by taking up tools and carrying them around with us as a permanent, ever-evolving feature of our being. Language was one of the first, most ingenious and probably most profoundly transformative of these human-making tools. Although the development of language likely dates back more than a million years according to Daniel Everett, its inventive brilliance still seems astonishingly advanced, still essentially unsurpassed in its originality, although now imitated or paralleled in various other forms—in the written symbolic systems of mathematical and musical notation, for example, and in computer software. Language is essentially weightless and immaterial: a system of shared concepts stored in memory and expressed vocally in patterns of sounds. It is an agreement to enter into a shared communal vision embedded in the covenant of speech—speech shared by readily identifiable members of societies and cultures distinct from other societies and cultures with sometimes slightly, sometimes widely differing world views.

I must say here that as time has passed I have come to think of the shared vision or world view implied in my language (and in what I know of a few other Western or Indo-European languages) as being based on a kind of delusion, a delusion of human species pre-eminence, of human world-ownership, of the world being naturally organized into an agreed-upon sphere of recognized entities like the furnishings of a vast human home—with the sky, stars, Earth, and all its creatures and materials labelled and arranged like theatre props around the central human actors, and notions of time, causation, ownership, hierarchy, and personhood embedded in the rules and mechanics of grammar. I think of my language as both a brilliant technology—a rich tool for expression and for knowing the world—and as a kind of brainwashing it is good to question. Why have I come to think this way? I realize that I am conforming to a shifting cultural zeitgeist, that I am part of a broad questioning of traditional Western culture that is underway. But that zeitgeist has not come out of nowhere. Key assumptions rooted in Western tradition and encoded in my native language have led to the wide-ranging extirpation of plant and animal species, the unsustainable degradation of the planet's environment, and the assimilation, homogenization and destruction of divergent local human cultures. What seems to be at work in the world—especially the post-Enlightenment, Western world—is a massive objectification of its many beings, a depersonalization of nature.

I assume that human language reflects and in turn shapes a culture's world view. Where this world view comes from in the first place is a good question. We can't know precisely on the basis of any archaeological or historical evidence, and I don't think it really matters—that problem can be a kind of distraction from the main issue—but I imagine that language is rooted in biology. As a species, however far back we want to imagine, we interacted with the world in particular ways in order to survive and express ourselves. In this, we were no different from any other creatures: our evolving system of communication reflected the ways our sense perceptions and anatomy positioned us in our environment, our physical fit with the world, and what we found salient and significant in our interactions with that world. Although I imagine that in Western culture, especially, the human understanding or picture of the world has become quite different from that of other creatures—squirrels or salmon, for example—I see no reason to assume that humans have had or now have a more accurate or complete understanding of the cosmos. Squirrel awareness and communication and salmon awareness and communication, such as they might be, I imagine reflect their different ways of being in the world. Perhaps in an experiential or metaphysical sense, knowledge of a microcosm is always a version of knowledge of the macrocosm. In any case, once a language or communication system gets established and becomes a shaping principle for a group of individuals and their culture, it does start to inflect the way that group perceives the world. For a long time now in Western cultures, I think, people have lived primarily inside a linguistically mediated, even a linguistically constructed, world.

So, language is a technology we carry with us for processing experience, and in *writing*, in giving words visual form and fixing them on a solid surface, we capture experience and record it. That's obvious.

The intention to write is in some ways similar to the intention to take photographs. It stimulates close observation, analysis, a search for patterns, relationships and processes—meaning, resonance—in the world around us and in our lives and our relationships with others. The writer intends to discover or impose some framing of events that reveals a recognizable truth, a shared experience that is not commonly acknowledged, a beauty, sorrow, injustice, weakness or irresistible law that shapes or colours human life but is often overlooked in the blurred and scattered course of experience.

But, as with the camera, in cultures like the one that dominates twenty-first century North America, language as a means of perceiving and knowing is in some ways restrictive. Words often function like line drawings. They isolate and demarcate things. With cultural reinforcement, they can invent things and set boundaries between one thing and another, while the unnamed world remains a phenomenal wave or totality without distinct or permanent inner or outer edges.

It's true that living things contain the fact of their own distinct integrity. Oak trees produce acorns that develop into oak trees, not into willows or tree frogs or rain drops. Crickets recognize each other and mate with each other to make more crickets. So, there are categories in nature, and it's appropriate that words reflect these categories. But it's also true that in nature creatures and things connect and blend into each other more fluidly than the nouns of English are apt to suggest. The tree is literally not separate from earth, water, light, warmth, air, gravity, insects, birds, fungi, and so on. And each of these named entities and processes is itself connected to or composed of others.

Words—even in contemporary English—*can* be used to speak of the world experienced as an integrated body, a wholeness, or perhaps as a current of energy inhabiting all phenomena simultaneously. Poetry often attempts to speak of or allude to aspects of reality experienced in this way. The art or skill in speaking of the world as an integrated or trans-categorical whole seems to involve working against the atomizing, disintegrating tendency in many Indo-European languages. Poetry uses language to re-integrate or fuse experience into currents or waves of perception and understanding, to offer multiple meanings, ambiguities and contradictions as familiar significant phenomena.

In any case, contemporary English in its normal (non-poetic) use as a technology for analyzing and knowing the world brings with it built-in assumptions, habits and purposes. It channels experience. It inclines us to value some phenomena more than others. I suspect that in its twenty-first-century North American form it is blind, or nearly blind, to much of the universe.

Although I am told that not all languages are as noun-heavy as Indo-European languages, my own experience of language is that the act of naming things seems to arrest or slow down the action of time and break the ever-changing flow of phenomena into separate enduring entities—an array of stereotypes—and thereby foreground space, making spatial continuity the platform of our idea of the world and time an ungraspable abstraction. We—in the culture I've inherited—live in the instant between past and future, but we can't figure out how. We insist that the present fills available space and only gradually becomes history.

Named things, with reinforcement from anthropocentric culture, can come to seem like discrete concrete entities whose interactions can be imagined mechanistically in a billiard-ball-like chain of causal encounters rather than as connected things, as changing aspects of an integrated continuous process. We name parts of the body without assuming them to be detached independent things, but we are not invited, culturally, to think of things in our environment as being connected and unified in a similar way.

And the most important way in which contemporary North American English reflects and limits our understanding of the world is not in the vocabulary it offers us for naming things but in its grammatical infrastructure. Subject, verb, object. Gender. Person. Possession. Past, present, future. Past perfect, future perfect, conditional. Active, passive. Accusative, dative, ablative. Here we are in the engine room of one very powerful, culturally constructed world, among its laws, as we understand them. Among its laws and dimensions as people have hypothesized them for thousands of years and have agreed upon them and entrenched them in our world-shaping, self-shaping technology. Minds and cultures grow upon language— especially upon grammar—the way coral grows on an underlying rock or a forest grows on a mountainside.

my beloved father was human, here's his hand holding
his knife, it's how I still remember him, I laid the knife
under his hand and covered him, my beloved sister
was human, mine were the last fingers to touch hers,
I placed this needle—it looks smaller here than it was—
between her finger and thumb, my father used to say
whatever eats leaves waste and hands are hungrier than
mouths, he said human hands are born toothless but
make their own teeth, here I am with my brush, and here
with the camera, beloved brush, the camera I'm not
so sure about, it meant a lot of arguing about catching
god, here you notice I've got it in both hands, very
human, and here I'm holding it in my teeth for a joke,
my father would have hated that, this pipe in my uncle's
mouth, see, my beloved uncle, was always a problem, only
animals carry with their mouths, my beloved father said,
leave the ashes, the scraps, the slash, the bones, we're
made to go forward, he said, that's why we haven't got
eyes in the backs of our heads or toes behind our heels,
here's my beloved aunt holding a pistol, my sickly cousin
with a book, some close-ups, hand with rosary, steering
wheel, telephone, cheese grater, matches, food dish,
beloved shoe, my father said never carry junk, remember
people only if you can describe their hands, them
touching you, some of them, hands want to reach for
what's clean, what's young, he said, what's past is
past, or maybe passed is passed, now, he said, is for
packing up, here he's shutting the trunk of the car

By definition, an experience of wilderness is an experience outside culture and specifically *outside language.*

The capacity to apprehend the world—surrounding reality and the self—directly, without linguistic mediation, without verbal categories or grammatical structures and yet with a perception of its depth and ongoing animation, is perhaps the capacity Keats referred to as negative capability. For the poet—as I understand the idea—this involves the capacity to revert to some foundational state of being, without language, and then to return to the linguistically equipped self, the articulate self, and *feel* one's way back into language, proceeding not so much strategically as spontaneously or instinctively at first to see how that non-linguistic apprehension of experience might be embodied in words, might be not so much described as enacted in words that radiate some of the character and intent (or direction) of the wordless experience.

This ability to explore non-verbal experience is also most likely one of the things referred to as intuition, which I take to be a kind of thinking through feeling rather than through language and logic. In intuition we react to an experience with something like subliminal déjà vu; we recognize situations and their typical outcome; something like smell alerts us; we read phenomena as though they are animate, endowed with known characteristics and habits—like humans and other animals—that we've learned to respond to in appropriate ways: quickly, instinctively, without deliberate analysis.

Poems, I think, often arise from this intuitive, preverbal relationship with the world. And because of this, oddly enough, one of the powers of the poet might be the ability to dispense with language— to spacewalk outside culture—to go about in the world clear-eyed, intact and mute, and then to re-enter language as a voice, as a kind of body, a living technology the poet occupies in an effort to convert the non-linguistic experience into words. In a sense this involves living in two worlds, being a kind of messenger or translator, being at home in the language of nature, the "language" of non-language, as well as in a specific human language.

Does this theory of language and writing really reflect how I think and behave, naturally, as a writer? Or am I building this theory as a structure for its own sake, a sort of sculptural hypothesis to be walked around and examined on its plinth, an alternative to poetry, with which I have a completely different relationship?

It's true that my relationship to poetry is shaggy and murky, not defined by clear rules and routines, and I need to keep it like that. I pursue whims, make commitments and betray them, contradict myself, hammer away stupidly at something, then jot things down in an unsupervised trance.

But I'm making an honest effort here to observe what poetry is and how it works in my life. I think there are many ways in which the language that I speak can be used to give readers or listeners the experience of poetry and many pathways to creating poems. While my own practice is largely a non-theoretical groping, it's true that I often do approach poetry by stepping away from language altogether to experience what feels to me like plain reality, the actual present, the world as it is shared by other creatures and by trees and rocks, and to experience my own being alive with as little fakery as possible—at times as a kind of dissolved witness participating in the world—and then coming back to language with relief to be re-entering this articulate medium like my proper body—one that can express, enact, imitate what I've felt and understood in that state of wordless awareness. This is how I often think and write.

Wilderness is what we humans haven't made and ultimately can't control, although we can influence and destroy portions of it.

Wilderness cannot be apprehended in language. To name it is to falsify it, mask it.

To describe wilderness—to report on an encounter with wild nature—is to plant the human flag upon it, to domesticate it and annex it to humanity's cultural domain.

It would seem to be impossible to write about wilderness as wilderness, to bring a portion of wilderness across the threshold from nature into the household of culture except as a dead trophy.

And yet.

And yet, as a writer, I am joined to language. It's a body I live in. I am most alive in the act of writing, and my impulse is to write about— explore, depict, interpret, utilize—those areas of experience that seem most powerful, most pressing and least familiar, least acknowledged, least understood. And so, I find wilderness, in one form or another, irresistible. The interface between my culture and the natural world, between my life as an organized enterprise and all the lives, forces and processes active around me, beyond my full understanding, is exactly what fascinates me. Wilderness is what I want to leave alone *and* what I want to explore.

This contradiction is unhealable, a rift, a turmoil that attracts my attention over and over.

Does the impulse behind poetry lie embedded in language itself, in an alternative tradition of resistance to language's dominant program of cultural conformity? Is it a vestige of a preference for a wider nonhuman community? Does the poet, the lyric poet at least, try to set language free outside the fortress walls? Or does the impulse to poetry lie not in the nature of language but in human nature, in the human need for honest expression? Maybe these two possible origins are really the same, and it's a chicken-and-egg kind of question whether human nature shapes language or whether language shapes human nature. Certainly, at the outset, early humans (*Homo erectus*, according to Daniel Everett) invented language, but since language has come to shape the culture most humans inhabit—certainly the culture I inhabit—and since humans have long evolved under the influence of language, it seems to me impossible to separate the conceptual imperatives of language from other forces motivating individual people.

I say this even though I habitually try to escape from language, among other reasons, to have something that feels authentic, unscripted, to bring back into it some discovery that wants expressing. I know I never venture very far. I go a little way outside the house and hurry back indoors and get to work.

A link between poetry and wilderness—a call for poetry—might lie in the fact that for many of us, perhaps most, knowledge of the self, as well as knowledge of the surrounding world, shades into wilderness, slips beyond our grasp. In the interest of communal welfare, in our shared public culture, this is usually ignored. Science, the economy, the judiciary operate on the assumption of extensive consistency, of there being obvious universal norms among people and in the physical world. We assure ourselves publicly that our potential knowledge of the world, of the human mind and the self, is limitless.

But in our private lives, in our spirits, our feelings and imaginations, many of us experience the world around and within us as vast, potent and unpredictable, and sense that our culture's complacent pretense of knowledge is false and inadequate. In death we return to wilderness, and in the loss of memory and the ongoing distancing from our earlier lives, from our past surroundings and human relationships, we might feel the fringes of our selves merge with wilderness. How to write about this honestly? To speak of this vulnerability, which is also a vitality, to express it, to enact it, calls for a different order of language, perhaps a music, a gesturing, that is ancient. The language of certainty, of scientific predictability, of a known and fully controllable world, needs to be broken through.

Poetry in this sense is always a betrayal of the established culture and always an agent of freedom and truth.

Poetry does not speak in absolute terms about the makeup of the world. It's a witness to things that surround us and constitute us which we can never encompass or control.

Poetry is honest physics.

In his book *Half-Earth* the American biologist Edward O. Wilson
argues that the only way to avoid environmental collapse and a
catastrophic loss of biodiversity is to set aside roughly half the Earth as
unimpaired wilderness.

In this he is clearly at odds with those biologists known as the New
Conservationists who regard the Anthropocene—the Epoch of the
Human—as a natural outcome of humanity's evolutionary success and
accept it as a new geological epoch in which wilderness will cease to
exist. Wilson rejects the idea that humanity has either the wisdom or
the right to henceforth treat the entire Earth as its farm and to continue
exterminating nuisance or useless species and engineering new life
forms to suit human needs. He instead calls the Anthropocene the
Sixth Extinction, likening our effect on the planet to the effect of the
Chicxulub asteroid that struck near the coast of the Yucatán Peninsula
sixty-five million years ago, ending the Age of the Dinosaurs and marking
the boundary between the Mesozoic and Cenozoic eras. Wilson explains
that the Earth has experienced five catastrophic kill-offs at roughly one-
hundred-million-year intervals, the Chicxulub asteroid being the most
recent, and that each time it has taken life roughly ten million years to
recover. Because life on Earth exists in ecosystems, Wilson argues that
we can't hope to save a few chosen species in isolation. Removing or
extirpating a single species can cause a cascade of further exterminations
and the collapse of a whole ecosystem. Likewise with habitat loss: "when,
for example, 90 percent of the area [of a habitat] is removed, the number
[of species] that can persist sustainably will descend to about a half," he
writes. "If 10 percent of the remaining natural habitat were then also
removed, ... most or all of the surviving resident species would disappear."
And the rate at which well-known species are now becoming extinct,
already close to one thousand times the normal rate from prehuman
times, continues to accelerate. He tells us that "within the century an
exponentially rising extinction rate might easily wipe out most of the
species still surviving at the present time."

He emphasizes that human survival is also at risk in a cascade of
extinctions: "The ongoing mass extinction of species, and with it the

extinction of genes and ecosystems, ranks with pandemics, world war, and climate change as among the deadliest threats that humanity has imposed on itself." The measure that he proposes to meet this crisis is a paradoxical human intervention: to *withdraw* from half the planet's surface and *leave it alone*.

So, Wilson confirms scientifically what Thoreau wrote back in 1862: "Wildness is the preservation of the world."

Sadly, however valid Wilson's advice is, it's hard to imagine industrialized nations adopting it, at least within the next twenty years. But what grabs my attention in his Half-Earth proposal is not its practicality but its bold graphic simplicity and its theoretical challenge. It treats a complex tangle of cultural, economic, political and ecological problems in concrete traditional terms as an issue of geographical territory. The concept is easy to grasp but at the same time so radical, so disruptive, that it fills the mind with wild surmise. How *could* we carry out such an enterprise? What changes would we have to make in our way of thinking to make such a thing possible? These questions have become a through-line in my thinking.

It's often pointed out that languages evolve in much the same way that species do. Like Darwin's finches, which have clearly evolved from a common stock into separate species through being isolated from each other on separate islands, speakers of a common language, if they are isolated from each other in separate groups, likewise evolve separate languages.

The source of human language's lifelike qualities is surely not that it's a virus that infects and controls the human brain—although it sometimes seems that it might be—but rather that it is such a subtle and responsive *expression* of the living human character and mind. Language is a tool, but what gives it its lifelike, seemingly autonomous quality is that it is a tool used and modified by many people through long stretches of time. It comes to us as a heritage; we learn it, live in it as an identity and cultural anatomy, use it, add to it, renovate it in certain ways, and pass it on. It exists only communally. We shape it, and it shapes us. It is a kind of shared mind, a cloud mind in which we all have our heads. It is not wielded or controlled by any individual or any single group.

It's true that, within a single linguistic culture, less wealthy and outlying social classes and minorities have usually evolved dialects and sub-languages and that the ruling or metropolitan classes have controlled the "polite" or "proper" forms of the language. But in spite of the best efforts of national academies, church authorities and aristocracies, languages have always been shaped by broadly popular, if not exactly democratic, forces. This fact, that language is not under the control of any one agent—not government, not business, not educators—but is rather the product of many shifting influences, adds to the sense that it is a living thing.

Change is a fundamental element of reality; so language has to change. How could it stay the same when nothing else does? But there are special human reasons for it to change as well. It changes to reflect people's changing social, cultural and political circumstances. Distinctive modifications of local speech usually begin on the surface of language: with changes to its music, its tempo, rhythm and intonation, with the development of a special (perhaps local) vocabulary—think of Québécois French, Jamaican English—along with special phrases and euphemisms. Regional speech often involves the development of special systems of verbal shorthand and elision so that communication can be stripped down and speeded up, making it gestural, a quick confirmation of shared understanding and intention. This makes the local speech unintelligible to the outsider who wants things spelled out at unnecessary (pretentious) length.

The underlying grammatical structure of language—if only the implied abbreviated structure—is usually the last thing to change in a local linguistic variant. Basic grammatical concepts change very little in any language from generation to generation. For centuries, until recently, the study of Latin and Greek helped to train students in the grammar and writing of the various European languages. My own study of Latin gave me a (temporary) understanding of the grammar of English and French. And, it seemed to me, key notions reflected in that grammar—personhood, gender, agency, cause and effect, hierarchy, ownership—had all stayed encoded in much the same way for centuries.

For grammar to change radically, people's understanding of the world also has to change. This might be happening now through the globalized amalgamation of cultures and the widespread use of machine-adapted digital communication.

As social groups change and reorganize for whatever reason (economy, technology, climate, war, religion, colonization) and as individuals move geographically and socially, language is obviously going to change. But language changes for other reasons as well. It's interesting to notice that within a culturally varied and widely distributed language, words, phrases and other stylistic elements are often picked up from its subgroups and worked into standard mainstream usage. Why is this? It seems to be like an ocean current bringing nutrients up to the surface from lower levels—a kind of stirring or tilling that restores vitality.

Adopting a few new words and phrases, like becoming familiar with any new technology, food or custom, has a rejuvenating effect. It's linked, if only ritualistically, to being young, when we encounter everything for the first time, welcome virtually everything and learn everything from scratch. This is one of the reasons, I suspect, that a surprisingly large number of elderly people welcome things like computers and smartphones. It's not just the convenience; it's the modernity. In learning to use new things, including new words, we feel capable, young and in sync with the times.

In many ways poetry is driven by honesty, by an impulse to revive the power of words by reconnecting them to human emotion and sensation and to the reality of events and consequences. Words can become tame, attenuated and anaemic; poetry wants to restore their animal energy, appreciate the evolutionary legacy they carry with them. Poetry wants to use words as live conductors to bridge the gaps between the self and other people, between the self and the physical world, the self and the inner self. This means reviving the energies in language, not suppressing them.

I've said that, as a poet, I often seem to step outside language into direct experience and then try to bring that experience with me when I step back into language. At other times, though, I feel myself invoke the power in language, inviting it to perform *through* me, offering myself as its medium. What intentions, what message or music will it act out? What I have found, in this second case, is that language does not work chemically or alchemically. There is no device whereby mixing concrete nouns, transitive verbs and abstract nouns yields oracular utterance. It's not like mixing phosphorus and water. There are games and practices for building word combinations by chance (slips of paper in a hat) or according to mathematical or scientific systems (substituting words for numbers or molecular elements) that produce surprising results, often chancing on brilliant metaphors and gnomic phrases; but this is all a kind of false alchemy, hoping to get gold from randomly mixed compounds. What looks like language's autonomous life—its independent energy or active chemical principles—is actually all legacy, a momentum imparted to it by the trillions who have poured their hearts into its making and have died, passing it on.

Language is always the expression of living creatures. It's their lives, their experience of living, their clamour and output that give language its life. The really potent and hard-to-grasp thing is that language echoes on, lingers, resonates with the condensed experience of the dead and the past in the minds of the living. This is what makes it seem alive. When a poet taps into the spirit and impulses of language and gives expression to them, what he or she is doing is tapping into the experience of past lives—an accumulation of lives, including nonhuman lives—immensely compacted ancient experience, the dreams, fears, longings, obsessions, conjectures, stubbornness, forgetfulness and habits of people hundreds of thousands of years ago, and of our animal ancestors calling out, storming with life, singing. It's their legacy language can release.

This recognition seems useful in the practice of writing. It alters the practice by deepening our understanding of it. Where I might at times conjure the energy in language and ask it what moves it wants to make, what exercise it has an appetite for, thinking all the while that I am experimenting with the medium, testing its range and stored powers, what I am actually doing is communing with an ancestral legacy, with the handed-on spirit of ancient life encoded in language. This recognition links me and my artistic practice not just with a technical medium but with an extended community. The urges in language which the writer can sound out and release are the urges of ancestors, forces deep in the self and in the living world.

Perhaps all that matters is that we appeal for words to come to us from a source outside our immediate control: from deep in the self, from the unconscious, from a legacy both human and nonhuman, from the depths of the sea.

Knud Rasmussen describes some of the traditional festivals of the
Nunivak Islanders in Alaska. The festival in preparation for the
winter seal hunt begins in November and lasts a month. The people
make new kayaks, new hunting gear and new clothes. They also
create new songs. To do this the community gathers in the dance
house where all the lamps are put out and everyone sits in stillness
and silence in order to help the men whose duty it is to create the
new songs. Rasmussen writes: "This is called Qarrtsiluni, or time
of waiting for something to break; for it is held that in the silence
and darkness, when all are striving to think only noble thoughts, the
songs are born in the minds of men as bubbles rising from the depths
of the sea to break on the surface. The song is a sacred thing, and
silence is needed for its birth."

In developing their own style of speech, people marginalized because of race, ethnicity, religion or sexuality display a defiance of the dominant social order and its judgment of them. This defiance is an unignorable strength, an admirable, enviable strength. The defiance of the poor and outcast is a strength the rich and privileged can never possess. They own almost everything else but not this—hence their romanticization of gypsies, shepherdesses, 'noble savages,' gang members, starving artists and black inner-city musicians. Borrowing a few words, songs, gestures, and clothing styles from these outcast groups is like wearing a whiff of musky perfume. It's an easy way to appropriate some of the outsiders' vitality—something less safe, less rule-bound. Of course it's a form of exotic tourism, slumming and exploitation. Nothing changes in the political order. White suburban kids listen to rap. Middle-age bureaucrats say "motherfucker" and "woke," but nothing changes. The minorities who help set the fashion trends of the bland majority know they have that power and know how they are admired and hated, feared and envied at the same time. The hypocrisy in which they're trapped is crushing, sickening to them. To be despised and desired and exploited: this is at the centre of the relationship between nonhuman nature and human culture. To be subjected to this kind of relationship against one's will is intolerable.

This page is always on fire.

Rather than deny mystery in our experience of the world, rather than push it away as a yet-to-be-illuminated dark zone or failure of knowledge, can we regard some of the unknown, unpredictable aspects of the world—and of our personal lives—as worthwhile in themselves, as sources of energy, powerful phenomena with which we have a relationship? With a slight shift in outlook, it should be possible to approach mystery with respectful attention and inquire into it, not to break it down and dispel it but to draw meaning and understanding from it. We hardly have language to speak of rethinking the nonhuman world in this way. I could say, "re-enchant the world." I could say, "re-sacralize nature." But these words risk sounding superficial or righteous.

An area in which many humans do accept mystery is in our attitude to our fellow humans. In principle and in law in most cultures, human life—as distinct from the existence of nonhuman things—is regarded as in some sense sacred, as possessing absolute value that needs no justification. Humans are accorded personhood, a key feature of which is the right to autonomy, privacy and mystery. It could be said that, at least in Western industrial culture, personal mystery and ultimate unpredictability are thought of as qualities that distinguish people from machines and from things that appear to be more clearly governed by instincts or natural laws. Most of us welcome and even require an element of mystery in our friends and relatives as an engaging power, a source of delight and memorable incidents. We want our friends to be surprising, up to a point: if they were fully predictable they would be boring, robotic, inhuman.

History and the current news, of course, are full of examples of human behaviour that refute this sunny belief in our respect for human life and personhood. Slavery has been widely practised for millennia; women and children are still frequently abused and treated as chattel. And slavery has many forms; the exploitation of the relatively powerless by the powerful goes on as always. And there are wars and genocides and 'ethnic cleansings' and countless ways thieves and killers prey upon their victims.

Another problem is that the concepts of "personhood" and "human" are elastic and often adjusted by people to suit their prejudices and affiliations. People have probably always valued first of all the lives of their immediate family members, then their community or clan, their guild or nation, their language group, their religion, and so on, in widening concentric groupings. The generic human grouping is of fundamental importance in the context of the nonhuman universe but relatively unimportant in the context of the home and family. In right-wing political culture, especially, and in identity politics in general, a central issue is how human rights and personhood are assigned. Extreme right-wing culture wishes to restrict full human entitlement to a select group on the basis of race, ethnicity, religion, economic class, and often gender. Claims for the sanctity of human life are tangled in hypocrisy. Social conservatives in the West use the sanctity of human life as an excuse for denying women the right to abortion and birth control while at the same time denying human rights to races, ethnicities, and classes of people apart from their own.

How can I believe, in spite of all this, that humans regard humans as in some sense sacred?

Wrestling with this issue I begin to think that the significant mystery is not the one preserved in the self, in individual personhood, but the general mystery of how a culture can claim to revere human life and protect it in law while at the same time, on many levels, the culture's respected members, its economy and its governing authorities are involved in disregarding and violating human lives. Perhaps this contradictory disrespect for personhood is a key to its significance. It might be personhood's negative—where it is withheld—that is most important to us. Those things to which we deny the sanctity of personhood we can exploit—harness, process, redesign and kill—legally and with a clear conscience. And those things *with* personhood, well, they get exploited too, but as long as they are not us, life is still not so bad.

There I think I go too far. Cynicism is an escape from thinking and acting. Somehow wars and the savagery and devastation of wars come to an end and people rebuild and trust each other again. Most people continue to treat peace and basic civility as the norm and violence and cruelty as aberrations.

In many regions down through history, travel, in spite of its discomforts and dangers, has held great allure; and among settled people, travellers have been received warily but also with curiosity and hospitality. Travellers enlarge their personal knowledge and experience and offer their hosts entertainment, news of elsewhere and perhaps new skills and ideas. Myths and tales from various cultures depict acts of hospitality not only as virtuous charity but as signs of magnanimity and strength. I can think of no myths or traditional tales in which the mistreatment of a friendly stranger is presented as admirable or normal behaviour. A fairly common motif involves a strange visiting beggar or a feeble old person or fool who turns out to have unsuspected powers or to be someone important in disguise. The message seems to be that it is best to be cautiously hospitable and to reserve our judgment of others: every encounter with another human might bring with it unexpected consequences. All humans have within them a portion of spirit, an element of personhood, which is a form of power.

In keeping with this belief, however hypocritical we might be in exploiting others, our laws generally affirm the sanctity of human rights. It's a normal ethical standard to respect people's homes, families, livelihoods and property. We endorse the public ideal that we are not entitled to confine, dominate or harm those we regard as persons or to force them to divulge their thoughts or disclose the mysteries of their personal lives—except, of course, if people are judged (according to the standards of the dominant culture) to be criminals or enemies in time of war. Then, like the rest of the natural nonhuman world, they are stripped of personhood and its associated rights.

However imperfectly it is honoured in practice, it is the *concept* of personhood that is important, I think, in approaching ecology and perhaps poetry as well. It is the idea of respect for the life, the inner being, of a creature or thing, the idea of its inherent right to its undisturbed mystery that is significant.

To imagine extending a degree of personhood to creatures, places and features in the natural world, to imagine respecting their mystery and otherness, their living character, and feeling a degree of kinship with them is, I think, to have a glimpse of precisely what is involved in the animist world view. Some form of animism—as in pagan pantheism and totemism—was common everywhere prior to the monotheistic-scientific-industrial eras and thus can suggest ways to transform our idea of wilderness and its value to us. Honouring the otherness and mystery of the natural world is no more fraught with ignorance and superstition than honouring the otherness and mystery of our fellow humans. A new appreciation for nature's sacred rights seems to be needed, since scientific data alone are not persuading us to curb our exploitation of the Earth.

If, as Edward O. Wilson urges us, we could be wise enough to set aside half the Earth as a sacred wilderness, the planet would again seem infinite and there would be little appeal in the idea of colonizing Mars as some people foolishly dream of doing. (If Western industrial culture has proved to be unsustainable on Earth, where conditions for human life are ideal, how could it hope to establish itself successfully on Mars where conditions are so hostile?) In the imagination, the presence of unknown territory is the spatial equivalent of unspent time—a future before us, which, to be the future, *must* be unknown. What is fully known has already arrived, and so the future needs to be free and mysterious, a wilderness beyond our knowing and control. To trust that the Earth holds a treasure of undomesticated wilderness is to feel that we have before us an endless store of life.

and because animate matter always has at its core
a soft quick, and brains and hearts need to be nearly
mush, the great currencies have all been versions
of flint. (Even the earth favours gladiators over
poets, limestone makes its bullion from thick
skulls and teeth, only once in a lucky while we find
fossils of flowers or tongues.) But those pure

hard tools for cutting and smashing survive the millennia
still clearly describing their vanished opposite,
the hot flowering beauty their makers fed and defended.
I claim this, that all the axes, spears, arrows,
swords and daggers were for guarding tender life, not
ripping it. I claim this. I claim this. I claim this. Shut up.
I claim this claim this claim this claim this claim this claim this

II

*We Worked Our Normal Shifts
But Whispered About Revolution*

The page as the forum for public discourse and custom is always contested territory. Those in control of government and social institutions want to hold this ground. They want to control language— edicts, laws, news—and maintain a social order and world view in which their power is secure. But language as a popular communal construct is never entirely under the control of authorities. Ordinary people always seek to inject practical truth and authenticity into language and also a degree of lively energy, which is a different thing from truth and authenticity. Official language, corporate and government language, becomes less truthful and energetic the longer its creators are in power or the structures by which they operate are in place.

In a totalitarian state where all the media are controlled by government or by a combination of government and corporate interests and where the broadcast news is entirely propaganda or a mixture of propaganda and advertising, the sense of cultural and linguistic depression can become profound. This was the case in the Soviet Block and the Third Reich for anyone who was not an active supporter of the ruling party. Many are now afraid that under Donald Trump the United States is headed in that direction. There's a fear that because of a rise in right-wing populism and the replacement of fact-based journalism with opinion-based social media we have entered a post-truth era. If we have, the period before us will be very dark and who knows how destructive; but it will not last forever. This is because, apart from whatever political and economic structures people erect for themselves or have had inflicted on them, they need language to have practical authenticity. That's why we have language: to communicate with each other about agreed-upon conditions.

Down through time there have been many lying emperors and priests, but no permanent post-truth era has ever arrived. This is another reason that language seems to be independently alive. It revives itself. It readjusts itself to restore practical truthfulness. If governments become totalitarian in the Orwellian sense and The Ministry of Truth is actually a ministry of lies, the language it uses will become debased and dead, like a crust or bark impairing communication, and new language will have to evolve to split that bark open and allow fresh meaningful speech to revive.

It seems contradictory to be arguing that language needs to be truthful and at the same time (elsewhere) claiming that words are inventions applied to the world and that culture is an agreed-upon interpretation of reality, amounting at times to a shared delusion, a habitual blindness to humanity's relationship to the natural world. But both are true.

I'm not an Idealist in the philosophical sense: I don't believe there is only Mind or a complex of monad minds inventing what we take to be an external world. I believe there *is* an ongoing material world of nature, of time and space; it's just that we can't know, for all time and with absolute certainty, what it is. We can experience it, but we can't definitively fit it into language and concepts. This is because we are part of the thing and cannot objectively comprehend it—in the sense of perceive it in its totality—and also perhaps because the thing itself is always changing. Certainly our view of reality is always changing. Our current Western scientific-materialist world view is different from the world view of the ancient Egyptians and the world view of the ancient Mayans. It's even different in some respects from Newton's world view, and it will be different from any view a thousand years from now. In every era people assume they've reached some final plateau of enlightened knowledge, but they never have.

Culture and language form a kind of template or a transparency marked with maps and names and formulae that we superimpose on reality to contain and simplify it and establish a sense of order within it. Reality is changing, and our idea of it is also changing; so we need both to maintain our cultural and linguistic template as an orderly agreed-upon interpretation and at the same time to constantly revise and update it.

One of the functions of art is to break through culture's template to make contact with the natural world outside and to revise the template, to question doctrine and routines. But since we rely on culture's authenticity and truthfulness, the role of art is as much to repair culture as to revolutionize it. Our language and culture are in a sense an enlarged and extended present—a moment we stabilize and expand into an occupied world in the midst of an unknowable future and past. Language and culture locate us in an ongoing narrative and give us a sense of having an established past and foreseeable future. In the same way that we need to constantly clean and repair our homes to maintain their space as a convenient shelter in the ever-changing ever-eroding world, we have to clean and repair our language and culture.

In *Across Arctic America*, Knud Rasmussen's account of his three-year-long journey among the Inuit communities scattered from Greenland to the shore of Siberia, the great underlying theme is the nature of humanity and humanity's relationship with the natural world. He discovers a remarkably consistent Inuit culture extending across the North American Arctic—a clearly conservative culture that has changed little over thousands of years. Groups thousands of kilometres apart who have no direct contact with each other are still speaking the same language and sharing the same stories, customs and technologies. Again and again he hears from people, especially from the chiefs and shamans, their belief that Sila—the spirit that supports the world—animates both humans and animals and that for this reason people need to respect the creatures upon whom they depend.

At the end of his journey Rasmussen travels with two Inuit companions, Miteq and Anarulunguaq, back to Denmark by way of New York City. There, from the top of a skyscraper, they look out over the expanse of buildings and traffic, what Rasmussen calls, "the stony desert of New York." Anarulunguaq sighs and says, "We used to think nature was the greatest and most wonderful of all! Yet here we are among mountains and great gulfs and precipices, all made by the work of human hands. Nature is great; Sila, as we call it at home; nature, the world, the universe, all that is Sila; which our wise men declared they could hold in poise. And I could never believe it; but I see it now. Nature is great; but are not men greater?"

Even if Rasmussen has embellished Anarulunguaq's words in translating and quoting them, it's likely that she said something along those lines. No doubt she was flabbergasted at the scale of what she was seeing and at the difference between the Inuit's restrained technologies and the vast supernatural achievements of American engineers. Apparently intending to celebrate the human spirit, Rasmussen ends his account with a summary of Anarulunguaq's awed and rather defeated-sounding sentiment: "Nature is great; but man is greater still."

But this was 1924. It must have still seemed that there would be no limit to the human ability to redesign the Earth in response to our wishes and fantasies. Today, nearly a hundred years later, knowing how the human population, pollution, resource extraction and species extinctions have all multiplied exponentially, Anarulunguaq would probably feel even more aghast and despondent looking out from the top of the skyscraper; she might observe sadly that her people's wise men had been right all along in their understanding of Sila; and the placement of the nouns in Rasmussen's closing sentence would probably be reversed.

It seems to me that the page is always a proposal or report of some sort, and is always in part conjecture and fiction. Our fundamental ways of knowing the world are sensory perception, emotional response, intuition, basic logic and imaginative speculation, but even these ways of interacting with our environment—most of which could be said to be biological or pre-cultural since we seem to share them with a number of other species—are influenced by human culture in the way we humans use them. To a degree we perceive what we are culturally conditioned to perceive. We interpret our perception of the existing world according to cultural norms. This applies even to our use of logic. We understand that conditions have antecedent causes: are those to be thought of as elves or as laws of physics? Are the consequences to be thought of as what pleases or displeases the gods or as a class of mechanical reactions? Is the universe an infinitely large clock or a floating island? Are the stars giant humanoid gods fighting and having love affairs or are they vast prolonged nuclear explosions? We project onto the world paradigms dear to our current culture.

The question is: how honest is the page we live by, how close does it bring us to the underlying real world, to the world our culture interfaces with? I don't know a simple answer to this. It seems to have to do with trying to use our senses honestly, with recognizing and questioning our emotions and trying to separate expectations from raw feelings. It has to do with identifying the distinction between what we have and haven't made and coming to terms with many things we haven't made that are natural—aging and death, for example, and the need to share the world with other living things. It has to do with patient observation and factual recording, with holding to the truth of events as far as we can ascertain them. It's all a matter of degree. We can never be omniscient or absolutely objective, but we can tend closer to authenticity and factual evidence or away from them. We can try openly to confront the not-made-by-human world or allow our awareness and energies to be largely directed by cultural factors. Shall we thin our culture's walls or thicken them? Will the page free us to have richer, more courageous personal lives or will it herd us under the control of some human authority?

The animation of language—its transition from technology to life-form—seems to have to do with the fact that it became integrated with the human mind and influenced human evolution. Humans long ago began to be naturally selected for language skills along with other survival skills and signs of vitality. The fact that this weightless insubstantial technology arose so long ago requires that we rethink our concept of primitive humans. North Americans of colonial descent have gotten into the habit of judging human culture on the basis of material brutality and the ability to manipulate and transform physical matter on both the micro and macro levels: to tinker with genes and atoms and to build twelve-lane highways and hydrogen bombs. But the extent of language's reification and externalization of subjective experience, the extent of its codification of thought and its aggregation and bridging of minds across both space and time—along with its portability and flexibility—make it still far and away humanity's crucial defining technology. We can live as nomads with language as our city. We can live weighed down by possessions and the crush of neighbours with language as our escape.

The page with its written word is already a bit of a downfall for language, a sign of distrust in memory or a preference for materiality. The page makes possible recorded history, libraries and codes of law, but it also makes material decay and destruction a frightful threat. In an oral culture linguistic possessions die only when all the speakers have died, and avoiding that outcome is inseparable from ordinary living.

What man with a framed licence and a ring engraved
    with a compass and
ruler has laid out the boundary lines of the oak's estate,
    its soma? In what
charter is the border between bark and aer, wrot and
    erd set down? The oak
spreads into the streaming light—phos, giisis, spires,
    aspires—and climbs
the condensed code right to the sun's brink, it's that
    tall, swims up a radiant
sugar cascade millions of miles high, the sky, the
    pneuma, the lyft streams
through the oak's pores, pours through the tunnels
    and galleries—blot, vena,
bloma—the street map, metro and hallways of Mexico
    City and all its
traffic are simple and small compared to this oak
    grown into the wind, into
the suburbs of air, the commerce of breaths and
    whistles, kreas, carnem,
carbon and oxygen bales, tanks, pouches, veins and
    aerial alleys, wrens'
routes beyond the ken of London cabbies—sinews,
    neurons, seines, signs—
and while they drink from the heavy dark, from the
    depths under old words—
bhes, sylf, slep, gast—the roots are not afraid to enter
    every room, every
thought you have, your dreams and trace
    rememberings, drinking
the knowledge into its growing reach, its
    gikendaasowin, its manas, munih,
mantis, you would never explore this one oak's forest
    if you had all

the lifetimes from Lascaux to Mark Rothko. And the
    light? Who
has measured out its border with the sun, counted the
    eyes it employs, the
forms it paints on nothing? Who has set the sun on
    one side and the sky
on another? And the water, the earth, the heartwood
    and me, my heorte,
cor, gaia, erd, my looking and being here, my eyes and
    speech—who
has put a border and percentage to each of them? To
    the oakwood in me
and to me in the oak's roots? Treo, truce, truth,
    zhiibine, du, duer, endure.

R: Is the page an authoritative cosmology that imposes order on chaos or is it a body of observed knowledge that requires constant adjustment to reflect the reality of mutable nature?

V: If we don't want to choose, if we say it's neither, what could it be? Even a diary, a logbook, a shopping list contains an implied assumption. I am such and such, the world is such and such, I need such and such. Is that cosmology? Maybe if we don't say what the page is it will have more range, more chance of adapting, surprising us.

R: Honesty versus logic? The freedom of evolving ignorance versus the paralysis of form? Can it be said that nature ages and dies in all its parts and after a time is entirely unlike what it once was?

V: No. That would be to project the image of human history onto something vast and mysterious.

R: Could we say that nature is alive and behaves with the purpose and intentions of an animal? Is it hunting for food? Is it building shelter, searching for a mate, producing offspring? Is it sometimes playing?

V: There is no answer to this since in its purpose, ultimately, an animal is as mysterious as the natural world of which it is part. Although the purpose of play is also mysterious, its breadth as a concept probably makes it one of the safest ways to interpret what's going on.

R: Is nature a set of physical laws that include chance variability?

V: Do you mean a law of lawlessness? A law that is sometimes a law and sometimes an accident?

R: Yes, but you haven't answered.

V: Why this interest in laws? Aren't laws agreements that safeguard the interests of variably inclusive or exclusive human groups? Aren't they reflections of the contested page?

R: Yes, but nature's laws would be fundamental to reality, antecedent to everything human. You're supposed to be answering.

V: Wouldn't those laws just be a projection of human mechanics? The dream of finding more forces to harness so that by flipping a switch here in the control centre we can make the Milky Way spell Coca-Cola?

R: You're mocking me. Is nature then a great human mind?

V: Not likely. But I think the human mind sneaks out at night when we're not aware and disappears in the trees like a deer.

R: Okay, you ask the questions.

V: Why does a question open territory but an answer fence it in?

R: Because an answer is code for "Stop thinking and get back to work," or "What's happening around you is none of your business," or "So there, Buddy! We're all laughing inside this really, really strong castle, except for you!"

V: Okay, okay. But can we live always on open pathways of awareness? Don't we have to rest?

R: No. Resting itself can be a pathway of awareness. That's why we dream. Ready to switch again?

V: Not yet. Is flippancy sometimes a way to sneak up on meaningful ideas?

R: Well, in heavy boots you can't walk as far. Can you say something that's neither a question nor answer?

V: You mean something ambiguous? That combines the two? Or slips between them? Where would that get us?

R: You say something random and I say something random and after a while we might find that a third mind or a shared mind is using us to construct something interesting.

V: Good luck.

R: Okay, what are the linguistic laws of perspective? What makes the page more than an inventory? What makes it a world you can travel in, deeper and deeper?

V: Once upon a time. Dialogue. Q and A. Paradox. Jokes. Anything with inward pull. Anything explosive. Poetry. Poetry dissolves the page and opens new space in the mind. Poetry gives the page three dimensions.

R: What about looking for patterns or systems in a welter of two-dimensional details right on the surface?

V: You mean like word and number games? They don't work for me. I'm busy in one spot, there's no inner space.

R: But isn't the page like a maze or fog in which readers unconsciously hide a reward they've brought with them and then enjoy searching for and finding again?

V: Yes, I see that. It's a conceptual version of an optical illusion: both a wall and an opening.

R: It's like inside the synthesis the old hypothesis and antithesis are still mating, and new unpredictable hypotheses and antitheses are about to hatch out.

V: But to open the page, to create conceptual distance, doesn't an answer have to catch—or collect the energy of—a question where its trajectory terminates and then use the question's energy or content to create a solid structure against which to push in launching the next question? I mean, when you pose a question the answer can't just come from anywhere. It's got to connect and conserve the momentum.

R: The only way a boring game of catch turns into a kangaroo in a shopping mall is if you catch the tossed question in a top hat that releases a pigeon and another hat that the pigeon lands in releases a cream pie and so on.

V: But isn't a game of catch somehow hypnotic—a way into dreams and out of our normal enclosure—and isn't reasoning mainly a way to tire the brain out so that it finally shuts up and lets us just look at things?

R: It's true, I'm tired of this.

Put your boots on backwards, pull your shorts down over your
eyes and let's go over what you've heard and said so far today.
Under the radio's rope bridge, under the news site's catwalk grate,
the gorge's torrent's noise, treetop mist—you were here at four
in the morning, your hands empty and nothing that showed
in a mirror but your clear-hole eyes, your mouth time-lapse
talking in reverse, back through childhood, through parents'
parents' cracked pale sloped thin muttering lips parting showing
more lips underneath, mouths inside mouths saying "world"
"wild" "wald," back through the plush-lined gulletry, earth-
tunnel-breath—all those long dead selves are still thinking
you. Clear-headed. Your world is what they see. Your eyes
turned this way and that by a girl with red paint, two quail
eggs and lamp about to go into the darkness of Pech Merle.
Er, ter, der, de, da, met, meter, mater. To be able to break all
the furniture, axe down doors and walls, burn the roof, roll
around outside with ants and asteroids and still leave a trail
of words you can pocket one by one all the way to your front
door—is its paint more weathered than you recall? your chair
thicker, heavier? Dinner does taste of some stranger's touch.

This photo was taken on July 19, 2013, by the space-probe Cassini during its orbit of Saturn, 900 million miles from Earth. The Earth appears in the photo as a tiny blue dot below Saturn's rings. The Cassini imaging team had announced in advance that they were planning to aim the probe's camera toward the Earth on that day. To draw attention to the event, team member Carolyn Porco urged people all around the Earth to wave to the sky and smile at the time that the photo was being taken. She gave the photo the title "The Day the Earth Smiled."

The Day the Earth Smiled. Courtesy of NASA.

I was dumbstruck when I first saw this image. That initial feeling has already faded a lot: I'm getting used to the image: it's becoming part of our cultural iconography, but I still find it very powerful.

It seems full of contradiction or paradox: it showcases the achievement of human technology at the same time that it hits us with the minute, finite nature of the Earth—our only home. It obliterates the notion that humans are "masters of the universe" at the same time that it extends our eyeballs deep into outer space.

But look at the spatial scale: the blue dot compared to the rest of space. And this is just a corner of the solar system! We are tiny, tiny, tiny, and totally dependent on this tiny planet. We'd better look after it. It's all we've got.

I shouldn't be so disturbed by this photo. I knew about space-based telescopes. I've seen images from the Hubble telescope: spiral nebulae, crab nebulae, vast galaxies of luminous gases, but seeing those images I was always looking *out*. I accepted the notion that the telescope is just an extension of the human eye. I took it for granted that the Earth was under me, behind me, large and solid, as I gazed out into infinity. The Earth and all of us—human culture, human history—still seemed central to the world.

But here, suddenly, the telescope turns on us, and I feel like a cartoon sleepwalker waking up 900 million miles away from his bedroom window in outer space. Yikes!

Or I'm like Orpheus who thought that Eurydice was following him but turned to look just in time to see her shrinking away back into Hades. Shrinking into a blue dot, leaving him alone in an infinite void.

Photographs are always about both the object shown and the act of seeing it. They implicate us, whether we like it or not, in the photographer's act of looking and the means of looking—the camera's mechanics and the photographer's motives, whether adoring or critical, prurient, grieving or documentary. Even an unmanned device taking pictures at random conveys the "philosophy" behind the photographic technique—the sense that events are random and disjointed, or perhaps that some mysterious synchronicity is at work, or that someone is spying.

When I look at this photo, I see the precious blue dot, but I'm not on that dot waving and smiling. I'm linked to the camera, I'm in outer space. And so the photo seems fraught with a feeling of *Farewell*, of leaving home, leaving family, friends, nation. Sailing away forever. I want an adjective for this, like *nostalgic* or *elegiac*, and wonder why we don't have one. Could I say *valeic*, from the Latin *vale*—farewell?

I feel such longing for that blue dot.

Can there be anything alien on Earth? Everything there must be our kin. Every animal, every creature and rock and molecule of atmosphere must be human. Or we must be part of all the Earth.

Could there be any wilderness there—in the sense of an alien, nonhuman region? All the wilderness is surely in the surrounding space. The vast uninhabitable surrounding space.

And we seem to be sailing away not only from the Earth but from *the human*. The photo was taken by a robot with a 900-million-mile-long optic nerve floating in a place I doubt any living human will ever visit.

In that way this photo of Earth is very different from the first iconic 1960s-era *Whole Earth Catalog* image which reflected what astronauts and cosmonauts—our representatives—were actually seeing from their space capsules. We could imagine them peeking out a porthole, snapping the photo with a Brownie Instamatic. But in order to accept that this Cassini photo reflects a common contemporary stage of human awareness, we'll have to accept that we have become dependent on robots.

The question is: what is essentially human? Are we a formula, a code for building self-replicating systems and structures—a signal like a virus that can be transmitted through space and reconstituted in various media by 3D printers? Or are we earthly animals?

I think of myself as an earthly animal.

But we know that this blue dot is becoming crowded with people and threatened by our incessant restructuring of nature and by our cast-off junk in every form, from nuclear waste to carbon dioxide, from nanoparticles of silver to synthetic hormones.

Maybe that's why the robot's eye is away out here. Are we groping for new ground like a rhizome or runner from a plant in a pot of exhausted soil? But if so, why should we think the Earth is too small for us—since we are so inventive and the Earth is so bountiful, having supported so much life for so many millions of years?

I wish we could gather some of the mystery and wilderness from the space around the Earth in this photo and infuse it into the blue dot to expand it again—to make it seem limitless and solid around us.

Leave them alone, leave them alone, the cloud-soaked spruce,
the fog-river valleys from valleys from valleys, the clack and
plink, shush and *hhhhhhh*, footprints in the ear, strides in the
closed eye

let them be, let them be, your children are sleeping there, buds
from buds from buds, yourselves as children still, your great-
grandchildren, your parents learning to walk, let them be, let
them grow in their sleep, arms and legs, you enter their sleep,
travel the sea and forest at once, dissolved in wind

breathing what you need, aware only of this

leave it alone, leave it alone

the ring in a box is there, the cup shining under a river is there,
the grasslands and the answer and the horse running away are
there, leave them alone

you fall in love with the earth again and your own life, leave it
alone

the cliff edge is there, the doorway of stars and the mountains'
blue silhouette over the river

the day without shelves or numbers, unwritten on, neither
waiting face nor listening animal, leave it alone, leave it alone,
it leans away wherever you reach, the ringing air, waxwings in

the dogberries, bear smell and caribou musk, leave it alone,
leave it alone

the room you've forgotten is there, your embarrassment, your
sobbing and sobbing, leave it alone, starting and stopping,
confused by what you hold, leave it alone

something drinking and slowly looking up, not seeing you,
something taking something in its mouth, swallowing, ripping
something and looking up

next summer is there, you don't know what it will bring, next
winter is there, let it come at its own speed

the rib bones, the leaf-covered wing, leave them alone

the rock somersaults into salts into tastes into veins into glint
into fur into buzz into swish into ice into voice into swish into
voice into swish, let it go

let it go

III

*Ten Thousand Teachers
in a One-Room School*

In writing about the limitations of language in relation to wilderness, I am thinking of the *experience* of wilderness. Since wilderness, as I define it, is outside culture and since language is inseparable from culture, wilderness, if it can be experienced directly and immediately, must be experienced wordlessly, non-conceptually, non-categorically. But few people apart from mystics, artists, spiritual practitioners, some deep ecologists and shamans will ever *want* a direct experience of wilderness. The closest most of us will ever get is likely our first months of life (which we mercifully can't recall), bouts of madness or near-madness, maybe great beauty, maybe sexual rapture, maybe serious disease or accident, maybe the experience of dying if we're conscious for any of it.

The *appreciation* of wild nature and the commitment to practical measures for preserving and restoring tracts of wilderness are another matter. Here language is involved in an essential way because fostering areas of wild nature in the midst of a domesticated environment is a cultural undertaking. And it's not just that language is needed in order to work out the political, economic, legal and organizational logistics of setting aside wildlife reserves or preserving wetlands and woodlots, or indeed to work out *whether* reserves should be created when these disenfranchise people who depend on access to those lands for subsistence or for maintaining a traditional way of life. There is a relationship between an enriched enjoyment of language and an enriched appreciation for the complex living reality of the natural world as both a sensory experience and a body of knowledge and ideas, a web of narratives.

This is evident in the legacy of North American environmental literature starting in the 1840s with Thoreau, whose best poetry seems to be in his essays and whose study and contemplation of nature is clearly bound up with his impulse to frame it in words and fit it into philosophical observations. Annie Dillard and Barry Lopez write beautifully about nature, and for Gary Snyder and a range of poets in Canada—including Robert Bringhurst, Louise Halfe, Tim Lilburn,

Don McKay and Jan Zwicky—language, nature and community constitute an inseparable creative milieu.

But it's in the abundance of writing on landscape and nature now coming from England that the relationship between language and environmental restoration is most evident. Perhaps this is so because England has for a long time been a largely domesticated landscape. What is left of wilderness there has long existed in partnership with intensely managed tracts of land and since ancient times has been integrated into the inhabitants' cultural practices—not only their economic practices but their popular culture and customs, their identity and sense of home place. It's a cliché but a significant fact that human history is a more apparent feature of life in England than in North America, especially Canada, where the focus has been not on preserving either Indigenous or colonial history but on reshaping both the natural and urban environments according to technological and economic imperatives. The British tend to take more interest in the heritage and distinctive character of their language, landscape and architecture than do the English-speaking descendants of colonists in Canada. So, it's understandable that an appreciation for the mysteries and beauties of nature can be conjured up there through the recollection of old regional words and phrases that sprang from a life that was once closer to the land.

This is what Robert Macfarlane does in his book *Landmarks*, where he seeks to revive "a literacy of landscape" and with it "a kind of word magic, the power that certain terms possess to enchant our relations with nature and place." Paul Evans is another English writer who, in his book *Field Notes from the Edge*, draws on a heritage of land-based words and lore to rekindle an appreciation for the countless mysterious and intricate lives supported by hedgerows and other, often small, wild zones.

I have to admit to being a bit uncomfortable with Macfarlane's lists of old words for the intricacies and particularities of the natural environment, and I'm puzzled by my own complicated feelings. I love the old words, their textures and sounds and the full-sensory pictures they conjure up of long histories of people living not just close to the land but *in* the land, deep in the life of the natural physical world, among its wild creatures and weathers. The words conjure up an actual legacy, not a dreamed-of future Garden of Eden nor neo-Palaeolithic lifestyle, but a historical reality in which Macfarlane's ancestors, just a few generations ago, lived hard but rewarding lives in much greater harmony with the land, drawing their livelihoods from it without exhausting, destroying or massively transforming it. The effect he intends is to suggest to his fellow Britons that this legacy of kinship with the land, this sensory pleasure in the texture of nature, is in their tongues, in their knowledge, and hence is a capacity and possession they ought to claim, preserve and exercise through preserving the wild natural places in the landscape.

So, this is all very positive. It's practical. It's a deeply meaningful way of advocating for environmental protection and species diversity instead of just complaining and grieving over the current state of environmental destruction. Macfarlane is the best kind of active naturalist. He gets out alone, hikes the wildlands, seacoasts and islands, and sleeps on the ground in every kind of weather. He's a sensitive, tough observer, highly original, imaginative, patient, personable, and a brilliant writer. His observations and accounts of his experiences have been excerpted by others and printed as poetry. What's there to feel uncomfortable about?

I think it's that this wilderness seems wholly accessible to language. In *Landmarks*, the natural world Macfarlane encounters in his tour around Britain seems to be housed entirely inside culture's barn. Although the barn is vast and ancient and neglected in places, and although the nature it houses can be more dangerous than a farmyard bull, there's a name, a story, some enveloping lore to cover every peril and mystery. The natural world of Britain is part of recognized history, part of legend, art, myth, and custom. The wild deer's territory coincides with human territory. The deer's mind is understood as a wild animal's mind. Its desire to run and hide and be free is understood as a wild remnant in a human context. There is no place in its range that is secret and unknown. Even its historical range, as far as it can be imagined, coincides with human history. The deer has been living with people in Britain for a long, long time.

Many artists and writers have investigated the attitudes toward the land and the natural environment that have developed in colonial and postcolonial Canadian culture. Margaret Atwood's poem "The Animals in that Country" is a powerful, concise exploration of the different ways animals are regarded—the difference between the identities assigned to them—in the Old World culture of Europe and the New World culture of Canada.

In beautifully crafted phrases she offers images of specific animals—cats, foxes, bulls and wolves—as they figure in European village life, sport, heraldry, ritual and lore. Her depictions themselves seem saturated with tradition, as darkened with age and convention as old paintings and tales. The fox is seen emblematically at the end of a hunt, "run / politely to earth, the huntsmen / standing around him, fixed / in their tapestry of manners."

In "this country," on the other hand, the animals are not seen as individuals or even identified by species. They are part of a nameless otherness. The language referring to them is blunt, graceless and offhand. The whole emphasis is on the negative: what is absent, not seen, not known: "Their eyes / flash once in car headlights / and are gone. // Their deaths are not elegant." In the Old World the animals "have the faces of people." Here, in the colonial culture of Canada, the animals "have the faces of / animals … the faces of / no-one."

I have long felt that this poem speaks iconically and precisely of my culture in Canada and of the general postcolonial experience of wilderness here. In Europe even the wild animals, along with the landscape, have been fully incorporated into human culture, into custom and myth. Their otherness is extinct. They are projections of human identity. In this country the wild animals' otherness, their wildness and mystery are still intact. Non-Indigenous culture has barely scratched the surface here. Our history is short and shallow, we are intruders, outsiders, confronting the raw powers of nature that have changed little since primordial times. Perhaps this postcolonial Canadian nature, without the saturation of European history and custom, is closer to nature as seen by Western science: raw, factual, without sentiment. Perhaps the natural world's real power and otherness, its ugliness and brute defiance of human values, are more openly acknowledged in postcolonial culture. This is how I first read the poem. It captures what I felt about my home as compared to Europe.

But now I walk a bit farther into the poem's thought. The animals in this country are being briefly seen in the sweep of car headlights. They're being seen from inside a moving car at night, beside a road or crossing a road. The road most likely comes from a city or town and is heading to another city or town, carrying the driver from a building's interior to a building's interior. And meanwhile we are inside a vehicle seeing only the illuminated road before us, which is a kind of tunnel through the night. The landscape, the forest on either side is in darkness, its depths and features unknown. If this observed world is a page, the animal that is glimpsed on it is a fragment of some symbol or letter from an unknown language, from a remote time, like marks in an ancient cave, perhaps part of a sign meaning "water" or "music," a fragmentary promise, a wish.

If I were not travelling so fast in this car, if I were to stop and get out and grope my way into the roadside woods and sit and wait until my eyes got used to the dark, things would look different. If the animal passed close to me here I would probably be briefly frightened, at least surprised, as the animal also would be, seeing me here unexpectedly. But I might be able to say what kind of animal it is.

And if I were to spend hours in the woods, days and months and years, if I lived nearby in a clearing in the woods and had travelled around in this forest neighbourhood all my life the way my parents and all my ancestors had, I would probably see the animal—perhaps hear and smell it—in familiar detail. I would know the animal from encounters, stories, legends, from a whole web of shared knowledge. Perhaps the animal in this country would have the face of a giant under a hill in an old story.

There is an ancient human history in this wilderness, but it is a history of shared and exchanged identities, not a history of human conquest and domestication. Look closely. Even here the animal's face is also human. But this human face is hard to recognize at first because of how it can dissolve and borrow other skin.

* * *

As an afterthought to this: it's likely that for the better part of the past millennium the most common British experience of wilderness has not been found on their island homeland but at sea. This is deeply explored in the writing of Joseph Conrad, whose background and sensibility are not traditionally English and who therefore, as an outsider or newcomer, is an especially objective and free observer of the experience of Englishmen at sea and the impact of seafaring and ocean trade on British culture. Conrad sees the sea as the surface of the cosmic abyss, a realm of wilderness which cannot be defined or understood according to human concepts and words. He shows the sea as inconceivably powerful and beautiful, an object of profound love and devotion, often violent, always indifferent to human feelings and concerns (which it absorbs and overrides), and above all mysterious. The merchant ship on a working voyage is "a fragment detached from the earth" and "a small planet" around which "the abysses of sky and sea [meet] in an unattainable frontier." The ship is a frail capsule of land-based commercial and cultural values—"the sordid inspiration of her pilgrimage"—which are often tested and profoundly questioned if not destroyed in their sea passage. The upending of knowledge and identity caused by this encounter with the wild universe, this sense of mystery, pervades all of Conrad's writing and makes it difficult to say how exactly we should interpret his stories.

The inhabitants of a land where the animals "have the faces of / no-one" face a stark challenge: the natural world is alien and indifferent to them. This could engender a self-reliant objectivity and a pragmatic respect for both the natural environment and the human community. On the other hand, seeing nature as unalterably alien and nameless can produce a culture that diverges further and further from its natural environment, a culture that evolves an ever thicker artificial shell and directs its energies into escapist fantasies. This seems to be what's happening now, not only in "this country" but throughout Western civilization. We strive for a technological utopia while our efforts are destroying the natural environment on which our survival depends. This doomed techno-garrison mentality encourages some people to dream of human life having a second chance in colonies on the bleak surface of Mars. Maybe the problem arises from assuming that the history of anywhere is the history of no one.

Dumb giant, I have no words to fit what I find on Burnt
Cape: joints of a sprawled octopus-size tree—roots or
maybe branches meshed with a moss-clump shrub, alder?
bearberry?—its tiny various leaves.

Or this end tree, the other shrub?

What looks like a driftwood stick—white, gnarled: I reach
to touch—is hard as a porcelain handle bolted down, bone
beads stuccoed into the somehow live grain.

Leaf-puddle tree flush with the gravel it grows in—is
the willow something the great gull of winter shat
from the sky?

Unnatural snake twisting up from a cold cleft into sun,
opening a mouthful of leaves.

It follows philosophy rather than habit, adopting any form
to suit its needs: trunk prone or upright, limbs fountaining
or burrowing.

Everything wants first of all something to hook to,
a seagull breast feather caught on a sedum stem, a father's
songs—a larch needle halts in the feather's lea—lichen
crumbs, moss dander sift in, a willow seed opens
a trunk of its mother's letters.

There is a convention among non-Indigenous writers in Canada—
if they wish to avoid controversy—to write little or nothing about
Indigenous people and issues unless the writers are working
alongside Indigenous people on matters such as treaty rights, land
claims and the legacy of residential schools, or unless they have
been accepted into an Indigenous community and can write of
shared experience rather than as outside observers. This is fair and
understandable. Even charity and praise, offered by privileged
individuals to those their group has traditionally oppressed, can
themselves reinforce an unequal relationship and serve mainly to
allow the bestowing party to feel virtuous and absolved. So, feeling
there's nothing they can write except safe platitudes without
becoming entangled in self-indulgent guilt, showy virtue, cultural
appropriation or ignorant patronage, many non-Indigenous writers
choose to keep silent about the presence of Indigenous people in
Canadian history, territory and culture.

But it seems to me that it would show wilful ignorance or at least
complacent naivety for me to go on thinking about the relationship
between wilderness and the page and the role of wilderness in the
dominant culture of this continent—to think, for example, about
the Canadian Shield landscape in which I live—without recognizing
that I've entered other people's home, that there are people whose
ancestors have lived in this landscape for thousands of years and who
no doubt think of it and know it in ways that are very different from
mine, who probably don't see it as wilderness in the way I do, who
probably see it imbued with a history very different from the one I
am capable of imagining.

It's true, I think, that taboos should apply equally to landscape
and the page. There are areas in both where we should not trespass
and where silence—mystery, restraint, respect, censorship if you
like—should prevail. In the landscape these areas might take the form
of sacred precincts, places honoured as belonging to a god or resident
creature, places marked as the site of some significant historical event,
or burial places sacred to the dead. On the page there are similar areas

which to enter without sufficient care and honest purpose—if at all—
risks degrading life and language.

But I don't think the Indigenous fact on this continent should be
one of these avoided areas. Whether Indigenous peoples north of the
49th parallel wish to be seen as part of a nation state called 'Canada,' or
whether they wish to be seen as distinct and independent polities, their
presence is foundational and central to what anything called Canada
could possibly be. Yet their presence has been treated as peripheral in
mainstream Canadian culture, a nagging side issue that many would
like to ignore. In spite of the Truth and Reconciliation Commission,
many feel that the presence of Indigenous peoples is still being treated
this way. I believe that being overly discreet and shy about Indigenous
issues only serves to further marginalize Indigenous people and,
perhaps most significantly—since there is an increasing number of
Indigenous writers speaking eloquently for their communities and
themselves—it serves to allow colonizers' descendants to avoid taking
an honest, responsible look at their history—it's my own—and how
those colonizers came to occupy and use territory the way they did.
How their descendants still do.

Broad disregard for and loss of Indigenous culture is the tragedy at
the root of Canadian culture. It's an absence and a shallowness inside
Canada. The natural world here in northern North America is not the
same as anywhere else, and yet we have European names for almost
everything.

Given that European colonization of North America did occur,
the great shame is still that it occurred in such increasingly destructive
waves. At first, at least, some of the immigrant traders and settlers
who spread out through the continent—the French especially, so
I understand—learned from the local inhabitants, were accepted
into their communities and evolved a hybrid Métis culture with an
uninterrupted sense of the Indigenous character of where they were
living. But in Upper Canada, the part of the country with which I'm
most familiar, Indigenous and Métis culture—already in some areas two
hundred years old by the mid-eighteenth century—held no appeal for

the increasingly imperialistic and mercenary settlers who were recruited in large numbers, often via the army and navy, in the late eighteenth and early nineteenth centuries. The new settlers were less interested in adapting to the local character of the land they were coming to, less interested in living *in* the land, and more interested in converting it into a semblance of the place they'd left. It became normal, here in what's now Ontario, to see the environment purely in terms of the resources it contained and to see those resources as an unrefined form of money.

Perhaps the harder we try to be honest, the more other hands take over our writing. Why express these regrets? For me it's not a matter of trying to win anyone's approval or identifying with a political camp; it has to do with trying to understand who I am.

The best way to get hold of this is for me to compare my experiences of Canadian and European landscapes. I grew up in rural Ontario with a strong attachment to the natural environment, especially a wooded ravine along a small nearby branch of the Don River. But most of my cultural attachments, the root of my cultural identity, came to me from Europe. This happened unconsciously. It came partly from my education, which was still based on a British imperial model, but it also came from within me. I found things in European culture and history that spoke to me of my ancestry and excited my mind. I sought out literature, art, music, history, images of architecture and landscape, images of life in Europe that had nothing directly to do with my formal (one-room school) education.

I loved the south-western Ontario landscape, I was born in it, I belonged in it, I was intimately alive to its moods and energies, there was no question of that, but starting in adolescence I saved my part-time and summer earnings with a plan to travel, and as soon as I'd finished high school I got a job on a freighter, worked my way across the Atlantic to Europe and spent a year hitchhiking around, seeing the cities, art, landscapes and people I'd read and dreamed about for years. It was a kind of colonial boy's homecoming.

The European landscape bore the signs of its ancient human occupation. I could read its history—the hill towns, the classical ruins, the dolmens, the painted caves and Palaeolithic artefacts on display. My language and sense of my evolved inner self went back through that landscape's deep history. The atmosphere, the character of London, Paris, Rome, Munich, Dachau, East Berlin gave me a wordless knowledge of the events and cultures that had shaped my world.

This is strange. I was also learning how deeply I am divided. Part of me yearns for this kind of connection with the Canadian landscape. I mourn the fact that I can never really or legitimately share in an Indigenous sense of the history of this land. My ancestors *should* have sought to join and merge with the people who lived here authentically, who had drawn their identity from thousands of years of intimate knowledge of this land. Instead they scorned them or disregarded them or feared them and pushed them aside. So, I have inherited the land as "raw nature." The history I learned to read here is the history of geology and biology. On top of that is the recent history of industry, mining, roads, power lines, logging, and farming. Around the old fields are stone piles two hundred years old at the most.

Where I live the old forests have been cleared and have partly grown back. The long-time first human inhabitants were evicted. There is nothing left of them that I can see. And yet their absence and their accumulated lives are here all the time. It is something general, something nameless I experience as I walk in the woods. Perhaps they have left everything of themselves in what I see.

When I think of it, my ambivalence and lack of knowledge seem right. I'd rather not hide from what little I know. I wouldn't want to be weighed down by Europe's explicit ubiquitous history, the land all made and written over by human hands. I want the animals to be wild, mysterious, utterly other and nonhuman, not figures from myth.

So, I both want and do not want a sense of personal ancestry woven into the wilderness here. I want the land in itself to remain beyond names, unknown, eternal, bound to survive human stupidity; and yet I wish I could say it is as deeply my home as the home of the Anishinaabe.

But I can't say that and so try to see as best I can with my between-worlds vision.

I assume that the old long-time occupants here read their history in this landscape more clearly than I read my second-hand history in the landscape of Europe. But perhaps even for them there remained in the creatures and land something wild and uncontained, a power whose surface their history lay upon or whose depths absorbed and transformed what they had been. I can't know this. The only truth in what I write here is the truth of my wishful speculation. But compared to Europe, the marks the old inhabitants left on the land here are slight or hidden from me. This seems to speak of their respect, their modesty and mature awareness of the human place in the natural world.

It seems to me unlikely that the Indigenous people's view of nature ever carried an overarching assumption of human ownership or that their myths and customs ever served to ornamentalize the land and animals by embedding them in a kind of polished cultural amber in the European style.

What mythology did I inherit from my elders and surrounding culture? What narratives coloured the weather and landscape around me? I didn't learn about Biboon and the Memegwesi as a child. I didn't glimpse Artemis in the Ontario forest or sense Apollo in the sky. What I inherited was a combination of scientific materialism and generic Christianity. The scientific materialism taught that there is an infinite complex of physical systems at work all around in both animate and inanimate things—systems to learn about, admire and manipulate—and that every event and phenomenon is the result of explicable physical causes. Christianity taught that this is all charged with divinity and also moral meaning because it is God's Creation within which humanity is being judged. The potential tension and incompatibility between the scientific and religious elements of this mythology were politely ignored.

Although the Bible stories, which the teacher read to us every morning, were set in a distant Holy Land, for a while at least their mythic import did resonate for me in the surrounding natural world. I recall, for example, in grade school, feeling on Good Friday that nature was stricken with grief and that on Easter every particle sparkled and rejoiced. The specifics of Christian mythology wore off for me fairly quickly, and I was left with an underlying sense of nature's divinity and beauty and my moral responsibility in relation to it. Perhaps this is common to all spirituality.

In any case, it soon seemed to me that what I valued most in the natural world was wilderness, its fierce and mysterious nonhuman otherness. I disliked hearing nature tamed in human narratives. I did not want to channel or ritualize my response to the seasons, to the rising and setting sun, to the stars or to anything in nature through reference to Christ or Persephone or any mythic figures. I wanted a direct encounter with—a respect for—the things themselves, more in animistic than scientific terms. I wanted to let myself respond to trees beyond their names, beyond what I think I know of them, sensing them extended through space and time joined with other life forms and elements we normally think of as separate.

Why this push into wilderness, this distrust of culture? Perhaps because I am stranded between cultures here. Or I am ashamed of my culture because of the harm it has done.

I have the luxury of that shame.

SELF-PORTRAIT NEAR THE
WINDOW FACING WOODSHED HILL

I am preoccupied and dishevelled. I recognize that everything I have written here about the page, language, culture and wilderness consists only of sweeping personal impressions, conjectures, and cartoonish analogies. I quote no authorities, offer no case studies—except for my own experience—and draw no deductions from statistical evidence. The idea of the page conjures up for me metaphor after metaphor, and I set them down one after another thinking I might be getting closer to some essential truth, some pivotal or multivalent impulse that might be useful as a means for initiating a range of creative acts. But even this vague quest is largely personal. I hope it might be broadly useful as part of the shared weaving of literary culture, but I'm slack and careless in the way I go about it: relying on my sense of belonging to a tradition of writers, talkers and thinkers, but also writing now as a recluse, more interested in gazing out the window at chickadees, finches and squirrels (darting and pausing among the sunflower seeds and pieces of bread scattered on the snow) than in trying to make myself heard in the world of publishing. I am reducing or returning the page to a kind of storybook world, a process of literary myth-making, an old man's nostalgia (and fake nostalgia) for childhood's make-believe narratives for how things work.

But here, in my stubborn defence, I now also claim that this intuitive naïve myth-making is how everything is built. The search for facts through statistics and scientific testing is always an effort to either confirm or disprove a mythic conjecture. Statistics are always in the service of some question or assertion; they might trigger an idea, a vision, but they are not narratives or theories in themselves. And it's not only the purpose for which statistics and observed data are collected that originates in myth: even the pieces of data themselves—the *idea* of what constitutes a piece of data—depends on a mythic concept, a mythic proposal. Words are needed to flesh out and give material particularity and substance to the heart-launched trajectory of a song. The song's intention, its current of feeling, goes out through space and time before there are voiced sounds and words. The words make the song audible and imaginable. Metaphors speak of the page in a painterly way, in a festive ritualistic way. Further analysis—if they deserve it at all—will show them to have been just a kind of drunken celebration or perhaps a useful way of thinking, an entranceway that invites more engagement with language and the page, which is one of the most valuable and durable ways in which we build, share, and understand ourselves, make our personal songs audible, legible, visible.

The writer might trust that the page they have written is an honest reflection of nature; but is the reader likely to embrace the page on the same terms and accept it as a reflection of their *own* experience of the world? Finding ourselves engaged in the world on the page— accepting it as in some sense authentic and true—is one of the ideal reading experiences, but this doesn't always happen. There's no point trying to list all the reasons a reader might find a page unappealing, but in the case where a page is well written and could be said to express the writer's intentions successfully, the reader's engagement or lack of interest often depends on whether they want their world view confirmed or enlarged.

But even a glass mirror showing some portion of the world will not be seen to reflect exactly the same scene—or the same message by way of that scene—when looked at by different people; so the page, which is not a passive reflective surface but often the product of individual expression, is even less likely to offer an image of reality that will appear familiar or true to every reader-viewer. And when the reader does find in the page an engrossing meaningful image of the world, it might not be the world the writer intended to represent or was aware of representing.

The page is an unstable compound mirror that shows different things from different angles. Its intention and message can be dynamic and restless. The writer might trust that the process of writing is inevitably the reflection of some reality, however controlled or accidental, and have little concern for what a reader makes out that reality to be.

If the mirror-page is always reflecting competing visions of nature, drawing attention to different areas of interest and concern, then the page is again contested territory and all its reflections have at least a subliminally political implication and take part in philosophical or religious or cultural debate.

Advertising and investigative journalism are never far beneath the page's surface. Here's an image of a healthy, happy modern family, an image endowed with a halo of approval, with a sense that what is being shown is a fulfilment of a human ideal—people living as they have always dreamed they deserved to live—but if the page widens its reflective surface in geographical space and historical time, it will show the modern family in relationship to its environment; it will show what makes possible and what results from its haloed moment. The wider mirror reveals where the materials that make up the family's home and car and appliances come from, where the minerals and oil and lumber are extracted, where their food is farmed and slaughtered and processed, where workers in other countries are piecing together their gadgets and clothes. And beyond the other side of the halo, the mirror-page shows the family's discarded waste, the billowing smoke, the effluent, the worn-out outmoded junk and packaging piled and strewn over the landscape, floating in masses on the sea, breaking down into smaller and smaller particles, molecules foreign to nature entering the food chain, crippling living cells, breeding monstrous growths under the holy family's shining smiles and clothes.

Every image, every reflection poses the questions: "What came before this?" and "What will come after?" The page questions nature as a physical system by journeying outside the focal present along causal trails. In the same way, it examines the social and cultural past or attempts to project a future. All this moving around of the mirror might be very unwelcome to some, very disturbing, very harmful to the advantages and investments that some people have.

The page also questions the nature of human culture and society ontologically and eschatologically. Every image, every reflection poses the questions: "Why this?" and "Why this way?" and "What end is it serving?" and "What end will it come to?" Is the page intended to cultivate and gratify the appetites of the individual self or to serve some external ideal? Or something else?

But beyond this I sense that every page, whether or not it ever had a reader or any social influence, adds to and alters the sum of human identity. This is a bit like the traditional view—the feeling, the belief—that the world is held in the consciousness of an omniscient God. In this view, every action, every word and thought of every individual human, even in private and in solitude, adds to the balance of human good or evil and influences not only the ultimate fate of the individual's soul but the fate and essential value of humanity as a whole. In this view, any evil, any spiritual slackness or dishonesty darkens the human epic, the aggregate human life.

The page is also a kind of puppet theatre, a cartoonish condenser. A child enacts the stories of the constellations or the burial of its mother by dangling a pebble on a string which meets with a seedpod rattling in slow steps on the tip of a nearly invisible twig.

The sign-marked surface, the place of played acts becomes the human interior.

This clothespin is Oedipus. He has been wandering blind for years and is singing his bottomless grief as an acceptance of his life, of all that's human. We crouch, watching this clothespin sing and ourselves cry with bottomless grief.

The language in which we depict ourselves and recognize ourselves is like limestone composed of densely compressed fossilized organisms now cut into blocks and used to construct the lobby of the office tower in which we work. The analogy is only partly useful. The organisms compressed in our language are not fossils but are still alive, although overlooked and treated as constituent building material. Compressed in the language we use are the lives of the countless people who shaped it and bequeathed it to us and also, beyond and within those lives, the energies and matter of the natural world.

The old words embedded in our speech are not old superstitions we have outgrown and superseded; they are still active at an interior level. They are living components in the media upon which we focus attention. An analogy might be the microbial and autonomic systems at work in our bodies. We rely on our hearts and stomachs to function instinctively, without our conscious involvement, while we focus on listening and speaking, in writing words and turning a page.

Inside our lives other ancient beings live. Inside our words ancient people are listening and speaking with all their hearts.

Our simplest actions and simplest words.

The jurisdiction of Canada is at root colonial, the development of imperial outposts from France and England. French and English, the official languages, and most of the other languages now spoken here have histories going back to other places, other myths and narratives, other layerings of customs and events. Most of the Indigenous languages that evolved in this landscape and contain the legacy of human life here are spoken, if at all, by a minority of the country's current population. It's deeply encouraging that an Indigenous cultural resurgence is now underway, with the result that many Indigenous languages are being restored to active use. Some, like Cree and Ojibwe, are gaining in strength with dictionary projects and pre-school language instruction. But the awful reality is that since the colonization of northern North America a large number of the area's original languages have been suppressed or extinguished.

My language, English, is a deeply encoded history on a transparent sheet that has been slid across this landscape and continent after the old voices were silenced or went underground. There is little direct connection between my language and what lies beneath it. I am looking down into the depth of the land and the past as though from inside a glass-bottomed boat.

I have to bore holes in that glass bottom, let the land, weather and old ghosts into the English-Canadian boat. I have to sink the boat, dissolve its hull, make English not English, make my words—ancient words rooted in Europe and the Middle East and all the people who have moved through that world—open containers, hollow my words so they can hold scoops of the world here, so that my language will register as English, be understood by all the English speakers, and yet be something else inside, the language of this place.

But I have been lazy, drugged with my family's heirloom lore. I have loved Europe and I still do. I have not learned Ojibwe; I have not even tried. Perhaps I've not done so out of fear of being rebuffed by the Anishinaabe or because I'm afraid of being accused of cultural appropriation. I value the few Indigenous words and place names I know. They feel like links to an underlying reality, to the deep land here, to its human history and perhaps to its authentic future. I also feel I need to work with what I happen to have, with what my immigrant culture has given me. I live in the great amnesia and numbness of my culture, and I need to work with this, explore it, not deny it. In my extended cultural self I have a vague memory of having come here in a drunken rampage, shouting and smashing things. The land has withdrawn, wary, disdainful, writing me off. It is still eloquent and sane. I am part of an unintelligible scrawl.

And yet English is entirely my language even though I am not English, not even European. And although the land I live in is stolen land, land my ancestors barged into, I do have a deep relationship with it. It is the substance of my mind. Its life, its presence, is seamlessly part of my own life. The exchange is like breathing. The communication is much more ancient than words.

Perhaps any language, if it becomes accommodating and generic enough, can serve as a universal language. And perhaps any portion of land and sky can serve as a human home. But I imagine there is a depth of experience, a richness of understanding, that comes only from having an intricate inherited relationship to a place, from having a sense of a history and ancestry that are palpably local, and from having a similar sense that one's language is the creation of one's people, their specific legacy, born from their interaction with the still-present, familiar, immediate world.

IV

Out All Night—What Do They Do?

There are many ways to define culture and nature, but a simple useful one might be to say that culture is what we've made and endeavour to control, or believe we should control, and nature is what we haven't made and ultimately can't control. Symphonies, cell phones, cities, and money are clearly our creation; most of the things that occupy us are cultural things: careers, news, history, politics, laws. We can take them apart and put them together again. Obviously we haven't made the Earth and its creatures, let alone the universe with its ongoing motions and changes.

While it's clear that the making of things and the ability subsequently to control them do not always coincide, I think it's important to consider the issues of human creation and human control in conjunction when exploring the relationship between culture and nature. This is because so often the motive for and intended purpose of a technological creation is the control of some aspect of nature. The fact that these creations often fail to control nature as intended—and sometimes produce new uncontrolled problems—is all the more reason to link the two issues. This is especially obvious in the areas of health care and agriculture. Scientific efforts to control illness, although broadly successful, have sometimes led to the creation of things like thalidomide that have caused unintended harm. The use of agricultural herbicides and pesticides sometimes has the effect of damaging ecosystems upon which agriculture depends. There is now the danger that we will create some catastrophic chain reaction—involving nuclear or biological weapons or the acidification of the oceans or warming of the atmosphere—that we will not be able to check. Clearly we need to pay more attention to the interface between our inventions and the natural world. A hallmark of Western culture is a belief in the human ability to devise ways to shape the conditions of our lives: we continually *try* to control things. But wilderness not only surrounds our culture; it invades it. Where we discover the things we've made are out of control or breaking down is a place where wilderness begins.

Notice that our bodies and our minds, at least our unconscious minds, are also not of our own making. In spite of medicine, nutrition, training and cosmetics we cannot control the basic trajectories of our bodies. We are born, we grow up, age and die like other mammals. Despite the ways we have been shaped by culture, by language for example, by education and inherited social customs, our unconscious minds are still at least partly wild. Our creativity, desires and impulses appear to be partly beyond our control. We never know what if any dreams will come to us in sleep. Stress and shock can change us unpredictably. In many ways we are still mysteries to ourselves.

If we are creatures partly domesticated by ourselves, partly still wild inside, can we ask the same questions of our inner ecology that we ask of the environment? Is our humanity at risk of too much exploitation, too much technological control?

I assume that the gods that people believe in or accept in their myths are often an indication of how they see themselves or conceive of human identity. My guess is that if your gods are animals or part-human-part-animal you do not see yourself as essentially or entirely distinct from other creatures. In the West, for the last two or three thousand years, the supreme gods have been given human form. In Judeo-Christianity the doctrine has been that God created man in His likeness, but it's clearly the other way around: man has deified his own self-image, especially those powers he most longs to attain—omnipotence, omniscience, immortality, infinite inventiveness, and the ability to mete out judgment and devastating punishment from afar. Since the Renaissance we've set out to attain these abilities in real practical terms through technology and industry.

It's worth noting that in the Judeo-Christian tradition God is distinctly masculine: the Punishing Father. There is no female representation in the Christian Trinity. Mary is of secondary importance. She intercedes with the Punishing Father.

The role of the Church in Western culture has been complex and ambiguous. It has promoted human exceptionalism and pride, although its gospels counsel humility and an acceptance of natural limits. In any case the Church has now largely been swept aside by triumphant scientific humanism.

The merging of humans with their technologies is becoming so intricate and intimate that it's hard to say what will be left of the 'natural' human or if we will become really our own creation, indistinguishable from machines. Science fiction and philosophy have been exploring this issue for a few generations. Genetic engineering, cloning, the merging of the body and mind with devices designed to extend life and to enhance perception, knowledge and communication suggest that, like the biosphere, before long we will become products of human design and artifice with little direct connection to wilderness either inside or out.

I believe that we made ourselves human by rebelling against nature—by taking more for ourselves than nature offers our fellow creatures—but now it seems we can retain our humanity only by accepting nature—accepting limits to what we make of ourselves. Perhaps the essence of the human was always in the tension between our limitless longing and our mortality, in our need to come to terms with this mystery. Perhaps the *difficult, necessary* practice of reconciling our desires and imaginations with the natural limiting conditions of our lives gives us a dignity and a kind of majesty that our celebrated gods with their easy immortality can never match.

Our culture is a shared thing, inherited, supported by many people. We live in it as a kind of aggregate, meta-body. What would this body look like if it had physical form? My first thought was that it would look something like Humpty Dumpty. We occupy a thin cultural shell with wilderness as the space around us and also inside. But the outer and inner wildernesses are continuous and flow into each other; so we're more like a sleeve, open at the ends: I picture a translucent, luminous sleeve-shaped jellyfish in a vast dark ocean. And perhaps an even more useful way of picturing culture is as a house containing a labyrinth of inner rooms and with exterior walls of varying thickness, windows and doors giving views and access to the outside. For some, this house is a fortress, even a prison; for others, more open to the forces we don't control, it's a light pavilion or tent.

I'm not sure my mind is located strictly in my brain or even strictly in my body. I've read recently that biologists regard the human body as a cooperative amalgamation of millions of cells which started out in our distant evolutionary past as distinct single-celled creatures that evolved the habit of joining together to produce a more complex organism with increased abilities and advantages. This elaboration of cellular structures has proceeded to produce the whole range of complex earthly life forms, including giant vertebrates and relatively small ones, like humans. Molecules interact to produce the organelles inside various cells, and cells interact to produce organs, and organs interact to produce our bodies, which interact with our environment, including other creatures. That environment, in turn, is part of a wider cosmic environment. (It seems to me that the way our lungs are involved with the surrounding atmosphere is not entirely separate from the way our muscles are involved with the capillaries that supply them with oxygen.)

In a sense, we seem to be made up of an interconnected stacking of intentions. I am assuming that the habit or instinct to survive, exhibited by even the simplest life forms, involves an intention of some sort. And I think the situation with a life form like myself is not that my mind rides on this complex cellular animal like a person riding a horse; it's that my mind resides *in* this whole aggregate organism, including a range of its surrounding environment.

What I'm familiar with—and assume everyone is familiar with— is a range of focussed attention. When I'm at ease and alone, I relax into a basic wide-focussed awareness, a sensory consciousness of my surroundings and my physical being. In this wide-focussed state I have the sense that my being, my self, resides not only in my body or individual mind but in the world I perceive. It's possible to widen this relaxed focus to the point of feeling diffused in the world, to experience the ongoing process of change in the world as the process that is thinking *me*. A Descartes-style summary of this might be: "It thinks, therefore I am."

But the self is, after all, also autonomous, and I have the common ability to narrow my focus onto an isolated phenomenon, a detail in my field of perception, or onto subjective experience, a memory, an idea, a plan, a problem—something imagined that is not physically present. I can apply strategic thinking to my subject: logic or imagined cause and effect or some formal pattern. And in narrowly focussing in this way on an imagined subject I lose touch with the surrounding world and my physical self to a large extent.

But—and I think this is the interesting thing—I am still engaged with the physical world and with my body on an unconscious level. In focussing on some isolated thing, I lag behind in my attention to what's going on around me and inside me physically, but I'll catch up again and feel hungry and tired and interact with people and deal with the business of living.

It's not just the alternation between practical living and dreamy thinking that's going on here. The environment and my physical place in it and my physical state seem to be pervasive and persistent even when I am not actively conscious of them. Even while preoccupied in thought, in writing something, for example, I seem to use physical reality as a kind of "language" or representation or expression of order. The natural world, especially, seems to me to be a touchstone for logic and truth, for feeling out how a thought or story or inquiry wants to unfold. What this means is that in the process of focussed thinking, groping for words, trying to clarify an idea or follow the implications of some feeling or combination of emotions, I widen my focus, look up from the page and take in the character of the real external world. How does it work? What is its logic and habit? I can't say exactly, of course, but it shares with me its influence, its solid normality and mystery, its movement into an unknown future.

In your face are tangles of strategies and logic. You see the world through that tight puzzle, and others see that tight puzzle when they look at you. But the back of your head, like the back of the moon, is wide open, a missing wall. At night you step through that open space into woodland and starry sky, into company with people far away. The shared outside world is the greater part of your mind, and most of your best ideas come from there like deer—or wolves—emerging from a forest's edge.

I have brought my tray of tea to the screenhouse—
damp June morning almost too dark to read.
Down the small slope there's the garden's unfinished
cedar fence I was working on yesterday. Gateway
posts at odd heights. The dampness darkens another
degree down, then down again, air blurred with wet
wood settling its weight, slackening like a slowly
opening palm showing a small pearl, a faint ping
like a fallen tree seed on the tin roof, a stretching
silence and another soft ping the same here-not-here
fulcrummed presence as the black and yellow
garter snake I found resting on the handsaw's flat blade
last evening when I was gathering the tools. Maybe
enjoying the sun-heated metal. Its straight-mouthed
utterly unfake face. White plated lips and obsidian
bead eyes. So real it could not be distinguished
from other things. I slid the saw out slowly
from under the snake, leaving it taut and curled
on the straw bale. Cold living flame. It only
looked at me, flickering its tongue. I too was invisible.

Why is it that we sometimes find the common style of a preceding
era, especially its visual vernacular, creepy and disturbingly morbid?
I find this to be the case, for example, with the steel engravings used
in the nineteenth century to illustrate everything from textbooks to
advertisements for fashionable clothing and household goods. From my
reading, I understand that from roughly the time of the Renaissance to
the nineteenth century, medieval and gothic art and architecture struck
many people as similarly morbid and disturbing. It's possible that my
fear of the Victorian steel engraving was instilled in me by the gruesome
illustrations of sick animals and cruel-looking veterinarian's instruments
I saw as a child in a huge book called *The Stock Doctor* that was kept
alongside *The Book of Knowledge* and the *Family Bible* on the bottom
shelf of the bookcase in the piano room. I couldn't resist peeking at
those ghastly images once in a while to terrify myself.

But it wasn't only Victorian engravings of bony sway-backed
horses coughing out botfly larvae that gave me the creeps; spidery
black advertisements for shoes, carriages, umbrellas and every kind of
Victorian merchandise had the same effect. And I don't seem to be alone
in this experience. Edward Gorey, for example, makes use of this same
negative aesthetic in his comic-grotesque fake-Victorian illustrations.

The interesting thing is that those practical, workaday nineteenth-
century engravings—so morbid to me—undoubtedly seemed modern
and attractive at the time of their first appearance. They must have
seemed full of the promise of new solid technology, new method and
expertise. I wonder if what is at work here has something to do with our
attraction to novelty and innovation.

People often seem to value new words and new ways of using
language for the same reason they value new clothes and possessions:
for prestige, to command respect, to claim personal space, to vie with
rivals, to be attractive and display vigour and vitality. Here we are back
in the realm of biology. These are all the same reasons that creatures
adopt various forms of display. Language, among other things, is a form
of display, a plumage, a call, a possession. If it is used in a competitive
environment, then, like fashion, language needs to change in order to

stay interesting and attract notice. What is outmoded and superseded is apt to be associated with failure, to seem ridiculous, even inexplicable and perverse. It might speak of a history we can't relate to or own.

But that doesn't go far enough. Why would yesterday's shiny modernity look ugly and frightening in the future? Perhaps the exciting glamour of modernity is always a deflecting or denying surface on the crude brutality of our lives. This seems depressingly critical of humanity, but we have mostly gained our living in violent, exploitative ways and, especially since the rise of settled and urban cultures, in the midst of disease and filth that we've had to brush aside and ignore. To enjoy life, to be strong, to think well of our children, our friends, ourselves and our whole enterprise, we need to be very selective in what we permit ourselves to see, speak about, and represent. As much as anything, this explains the devotion to progress. It's a belief in better selves that excuses the present.

So, the 'modern look' is a way of being upbeat, positive, progressive, self-respecting. It's a screen concealing or turning attention away from slavery, butchery, rape, poverty, exploitation, neglect, disease, shit, rot, decrepitude and death. It's true that the process of modernization has reduced the amount of some of these things, but often the effect has been merely to distance them or give them a new form. With the passage of time, as attention turns to new forms of modernity, new distractions, the old "modern" vernaculars look threadbare and soiled; we see them not as screens that conceal horrors or as a promise to end them but as direct links to the old horrors themselves.

Looking back, from the perspective of the present, the gap between the decent and the indecent collapses. The more polite and progressive the style of the time was—or the more God-fearing and righteous—the more we now see it as a symptom of its opposite. All the night terrors it once concealed are now on the surface.

I believe C.G. Jung was right in arguing that there is such a thing as a collective unconscious *and* that it is nothing more than instinctive mind. It's clear our bodies have evolved with built-in instinctive behaviours—everything from digestion to healing to aging, all of which go on mostly without our conscious control. Why imagine that our minds are somehow different and lack equivalent, inherited, autonomic behaviours?

It seems obvious to me that much of what our minds do *is* unconscious, that we share these unconscious processes with each other *and* with other creatures, and that these processes are linked to processes in nature: that's how they evolved.

We do think with a mind beyond ourselves: a wild, aggregate mind.

I sometimes think of sleep as coming up for air—the reverse of how we generally conceive of our daytime and nighttime experience. Maybe we're like scuba divers in our waking lives, holding a charge of *chi* or wild energy as long as we can as we go about our individual daily activities; then surfacing, shedding the wetsuits of our public personalities (all the responsibilities and projects) and re-entering the ancient homeland of sleep where we merge freely with the forces of nature and take on another day's worth of energy.

Hello, white goose beauty pain.
Bundle fire, yes, I have it.
Tree hair, yes, I have it.
The dead child fingers fast feather music under the rocks
over there.
Fast mice finger sunrise face, she eats and grows tall.
Stitching a long, long bluebird and canary cape.
Sit down here, I will open the bundle.

Before words were tamed and herded together into the enclosure of the page, they each had their own homes and favoured haunts out in the landscape. Some lived in the branches of trees, some in rocks and cliffs, some in running water, some in wind, some slept in burrows, some in women, some in men, in the eyes' pupils, in knife blades, in the stomach's hunger.

The most important words, the strong words, were easily recognized, easily remembered sounds you could think of at any time but might encounter first-hand in your daily rounds as the world was still or changing around you. The words were sounds that marked the sites where strong creatures lived, where they might appear and change everything, announce you were in their territory, alter the air, make it blissful or frightening, make you love or sleep or raging mad.

The words were the names of gods and also the names of the sites where you were likely to encounter them, the places and the situations, the emerging events, the interactions with others, the behaviours and expressions of other people, which are also places no different than springs or caves. The words marked the sites in the world where the gods' powers leapt out, where you stepped into those powers, those personalities, and their rule over you. The words marked the map of the world where lightning had struck—various kinds of lightning— and where it would likely strike again when you went there. The sounds of the words themselves, their feel in the mouth, the breath they were made from and the way they could come into view in thought, silently as reminders, were portions of the gods' energies, tastes of the lightning itself.

The world these words lived in was both map and landscape. It was a song or story and a world of creatures and events that you walked through, that you engaged with, every day. The word-map was given life by the outdoor world and fused with it. Where the words lived was where the gods lived, which was the same world where the brook lived and where the crow and the pine lived.

The landscape had various paths—over its surface as well as into it and through it and out of it. Love was in the landscape, and hatred and jealousy and sickness and enemies' violence and birth and death, all along pathways, through tunnels and clearings into encounters with the gods we remembered by name.

Remembering them by name and where they were likely to be met and teaching this map to our children and sharing it among ourselves made us human. We were the ones walking around with the gods in our mouths, in our breath, holding the world they owned in a net of sounds we could share. We made the gods into puppets of sound and played with them, as a group, as a people, on a stage we made in concert with one another.

That lightning was the first thing we tamed.

That lightning map was the first home we built.

The gods were now our emotions and thoughts. What we pictured inside ourselves with our eyes closed. And when we herded the words together out of their homes in the tunnelled and crisscrossed landscape, when we put them in a pen on the floor in a covered place and said, "This is a page, this inside place stands for all that's outside," we invented a new version of mind.

We tend to think of emotion as an amorphous subjective sensation, a rush of physical feeling arising from within, a wash of colour as compared to the precise linear outline of logic or a known fact. But perhaps emotion is the oldest knowledge, the deepest registry of the self and the self's most ancient way of recording and categorizing the kinds of effect the external world can provide and the kinds of response the external world can elicit in the self. By "the self" we might think of any unit of life, any perceiving entity, a marine organism, an insect, a plant, a mammal. We can think of emotion as pre-rational knowledge, instinctive knowledge. It is knowledge that directly engages and mobilizes the physical systems of the body without consulting the judiciary of the mind. Emotions are the whole body working as mind, which must be how life has functioned for hundreds of millions of years. The world is defined by a range of features that trigger desire, fear, combative rage, compassionate empathy, tenderness, possessiveness, suspicion, revulsion, exultation, bliss.

Those of us who live in a controlled, fabricated world defined by language and material technology have come to believe that we should be responsible for emotional knowledge, that we should be able to shape and control it in the same way that we shape and control time and our physical environment—our daily and yearly activities, our getting of food and shelter, our social interactions. But emotional knowledge has remained wild and uncultured in a way, and our uneasy relationship with it—in the midst of our rooms and clothes and machinery—is apt to make us feel sick.

For one thing, in an artificial environment where the phenomenal world is largely the product of human intentions, where everything carries human messages, human uses and signals, in such a world the self's instinctive emotional response to the environment becomes confused and overloaded and needs to be ignored or shut down. The emotional messages in a city might be layered and complex, and this alone gives the impression that emotions are often vague, imprecise, mushy and murky rather than clear and hard—flushes, rushes, flashes of contradictory feeling instead of the building material of factual information. And yet we continue to think of emotions—which probably constitute our most primitive way of knowing the world, the most instinctual and in a sense mechanical response to the world—as the quality of experience that differentiates humans from machines. We might invent artificial intelligence, but we doubt that we will ever invent artificial emotion.

People who experience their emotions as objective external phenomena or as always caused by external agents are seen as insane, often dangerously deviant. These are the classic symptoms of projection and paranoid schizophrenia. But perhaps at an earlier point in our history this link between emotion and environment was more the norm. This raises interesting questions about the experience of wilderness, including the experience of the natural world outside—or at least partly outside—the framework of culture. Is the experience of wilderness, from the acculturated human point of view, inevitably an experience of insanity?

The experience of the shaman has always been a matter of going out from the cultural community into the wilderness—also thought of as a realm of spirits—and returning with knowledge and power of some kind that can help the human community. In various ways this has also been the role of the priest, the poet, and the artist in general. And it's an old truism that madness and creativity have something in common. The artist steps outside culturally categorical ways of thinking and perceiving, draws on "wild" energy and knowledge, and infuses that into a creation of some kind that helps to renew and revitalize human culture.

Perhaps the "pathetic fallacy" of attributing human emotion and reciprocity to the natural environment is not so much a fallacy as a continuity of ancient emotional knowledge and a common feature of madness, mysticism, shamanism, the poetic approach to language, and other experiences in which the self is exposed to wilderness. Perhaps emotional knowledge looks like a pathetic fallacy only from the standpoint of the stolid cultural enclave in which it is assumed that all mental experience is interior and autonomous.

Perhaps wariness about anthropomorphism—which is surely valid if we think of anthropomorphism as the projection of human cultural values and customs onto nature—is also misplaced on a deeper level. What if we think of the cultural mind as a kind of hollow rubber ball with its subjective experience on the inside? What if we make a slit in that ball and turn it inside out so that the outside world washes over the former centre and the subjective contents are now on the external surface where the outside world is directly in contact with them, mingled with them? I imagine this is close to the experience of wilderness and the self's experience of the world in an acultural state. The self is dispersed, it has its life *in* the surrounding phenomena as part of the environment, as part of a network of active creatures and elements. Experience then is not a matter of projecting emotions and values into external things but of actually participating in those things, being constituted by them.

We distinguish among kinds of sensory perception. When we see an object—an oak tree, a mountain—we discern that the object has a reality distinct from our bodies, our 'selves.' We make an exception for emotional knowledge—those of us who are sane and getting along with our cultural community and not poets raving in private—we behave as though what we are experiencing emotionally is confined "inside us," to our inner selves. We don't scream and point at things no one else can see. But we are surrounded by and pervaded by emotional triggers, spirits that we learn politely to ignore.

The page is a culturally acceptable way of harnessing and trading in these spirits. A person laughing at a page or crying at a page is not considered insane. Words conjure emotions and imaginary events which are given semi-free rein inside the cultural enclave. In this way the page can offer a *taste* of wilderness, a semblance of what it is, without going outside.

In the ancient world, the forces that struck the self with emotion, flooded the self with emotion, were considered gods. Conversely, emotions were the touches the self received from gods residing in the surrounding world: gods of desire, rage, fear, etcetera. These gods had their homes, their perches and precincts and situations and traps. Where they were likely to be encountered made up a map of the world. The world was known through emotional knowledge. There was the god of love along that path. Maybe you could see it up ahead and avoid it if you wanted to, or maybe you fell for it again and had no choice. Or you ran toward it. Or you were oblivious, or thought you were walking a different path, and the god whacked you or stole you away.

The page is the door of a little house outside which a god lives. Will you open the door and let the god strike you? Every kind of god you can imagine is behind the page. They are effigies, these gods, but if you address them and let them address you, they will give you direct emotional knowledge from outside your hill-fort town.

What kind of knowledge does someone bring from an experience of wilderness—from an experience of homelessness, from having lost the self-as-inside and known it as outside, impersonal, dispersed, without location, without beginning or end? It is, I think, finally a knowledge of joy. Joy as the energy inside being, the awareness of being.

Wilderness is made up of constant movement, constant change, which means individual things dying that do not want to die and individual things being born that exult in being alive, and this constant combined process, this life made up of birth and death, is what the self embraces in wilderness, and its fierce energy and joy is what the poet can bring back to people bent over and focussed on the consequences of each gain and loss, on the reprieve and demands of each birth, the loss and opportunity of each death. The human heart wearies, gripping things like that.

As Chagall reminds us, there are among us and within us versions of ourselves who travel far away from our daily world, who live part-time somewhere else but are also always nearby—on a rooftop a green-faced man in a purple coat is playing a violin, a red bird-fish woman with flowers is blowing a horn—they pour joy into our starved hearts if we stop, look their way, and listen.

Another way in which I sometimes think of poetry is this: not a re-wilding of speech nor an invitation to be "spoken through" by language, but as a state of awareness that can be induced by language and in which we feel engaged and perhaps reconciled with what is real and larger than the self. At its core, poetry might be a kind of excitement, a sense of recognition, discovery or marvelling. Other arts and practices also can bring us to poetry in this sense.

It's interesting that some of the poetry I find most powerful, most effective in generating an expanded state of awareness, consists of plain, factual statements and a use of language that on the surface at least seems indistinguishable from ordinary utilitarian prose. This is at work in Catullus's poem "101" in memory of his dead brother: "Driven across many nations, across many oceans, / I am here, my brother, for this final parting, /…" Likewise, the language itself is remarkably factual and unadorned in this well-known poem from William Carlos Williams's *Spring and All*:

> so much depends
> upon
>
> a red wheel
> barrow
>
> glazed with rain
> water
>
> beside the white
> chickens

But here our attention is slowed and focussed by the way the enigmatic pictorial statement is broken into four sparse two-line stanzas, each with a two-beat line haltingly followed by a one-beat line. The plain language heats up, however, because of two conflicting forces. The opening "so much depends / upon" generates a forward momentum, a desire in the reader to find the answer and complete the proposition, but the structure of the poem then impedes the momentum, and the effect is something like electrical energy passing through a resistance coil and heating it up. The fact that the poem begins with an abstract promise (here's what so much depends upon...) and answers that with an incongruous image of a wheelbarrow and chickens adds to the sense of an unresolved, undissipated charge of energy or aura of meaning.

Prose translations of foreign language poetry often seem to me to carry a real poetic charge. This is what I liked about the old Penguin books of foreign verse in which the poems were printed in their original language and form and then followed at the bottom of the page by an English prose translation in a smaller font. I often found I preferred those prose translations to any efforts to translate the poems into English poetry.

Perhaps it's because I've learned to recognize and respond to poetry as a special, alternative use of language that I sometimes respond to apparently ordinary language as poetry. Perhaps it's a matter of context and expectation: if I expect that what I'm hearing or reading is a poem, I will allow it to work on me, at least initially, as a poem; I will be open to—hopeful for—the possibility that I might discover a new kind of poetry, an unfamiliar use of language that is exciting and revealing in new ways. But at the same time (we surely all do this), I respond to poetry as a performance; I want to enjoy it, but at the same time I receive it through a critical filter. For ordinary language to work as poetry, it must maintain an inner tension, it must seem honest and necessary; I need to trust that it serves a clear, hard expressive intention. No pointless repetition, no clichés, no empty posturing or automatic blather. Unlike poetry, ordinary language tends to run on according to colloquial conventions and its own boring momentum.

I like the prose translations of poetry, sometimes, because I know I'm dealing with poetry, and the plain prose seems to give me the heart or bare bones of the poem. My imagination can work with that. The plain language in Catullus's poem seems to me austere and honest, humble, universal, and personal, timeless in the face of death. The plain language in Williams's poem seems charged with meaning because of the way he sets it up, because of the range of other poetic techniques in which it's embedded. And I think this is instructive. In responding to the blunt, concrete language in "so much depends," I'm not responding to plain, spontaneous, prosaic speech; I'm responding to a device, to words used in a highly artificial way.

In the act of naming phenomena and fitting them into the template of grammar, writing plants the human flag on nature, categorizes and evaluates it, and the human mind domesticates it, annexes it into the empire of culture. But poetry attempts to loosen this way of knowing the world. It's as though instead of killing and stuffing an animal and bringing it back to decorate a hall, poetry attempts—or pretends—to go out into the field to be amongst the animals and know them *in* the wild. Questioning discrete facts, poetry explores ambiguities, layered meanings, hints, uncertainties, paradoxes, mixtures, and transitions. It revives a sense of the freshness and newness of experience just *before* we have categorized it and filed it away.

A key poetic device that thins our culture's conceptual walls and opens us to new experience is metaphor. Metaphor involves making verbal connections that could be thought of as corresponding to new synaptic circuits in the brain, new ways of understanding relationships in the world and in ourselves. It involves a "carrying across," a "transfer" as the original Greek μεταφέρειν (*metapherein*) implies: a transfer as though across a bridge from the familiar *here* or *inside* to the newly discovered *beyond*.

What I find equally interesting is a kind of balked or refracted (or perplexed) metaphor that occurs in paradox and contradiction where the transfer or carrying across of understanding begins but is then suspended as though halfway over a gulf at the edge of a broken bridge. This suspension of transfer might occur in a word-package such as an oxymoron but is often produced when the train of thought or sequence of perceptions in a poem circles around and produces an implicit contradiction or paradox. The effect of this is to reveal the limits of logic and language themselves in apprehending reality.

The poetry of John Donne and George Herbert, for example, abounds in paradox and perplexed metaphors. Herbert's "The Collar" dramatizes his angry private rebellion against the restrictions of his religious vocation symbolized by his clerical collar. The collar used here as symbol and title is complex: the word contains a triple entendre through the implied homophones 'caller' and 'choler.' Herbert's passionate argument for personal, worldly freedom and fulfilment—his loud 'choler' which goes on for twenty-nine lines—is suddenly silenced by a quiet but more powerful inner voice or 'caller.' His outburst of frustration has led to a seemingly contradictory renewal of faith and devotion. The poem ends like this:

> "He that forbears
> To suit and serve his need
> Deserves his load."
> But as I raved, and grew more fierce and wild
> At every word,
> Methoughts I heard one calling, "Child!"
> And I replied, "My Lord!"

Donne's "Holy Sonnet 14" is somewhat similar in theme and makes more overt use of contradictory metaphors of freedom in imprisonment and chastity in ravishment. He calls on his God: "Take me to You, imprison me, for I / Except You enthrall me, never shall be free; / Nor ever chaste, except You ravish me."

What poetry tends to aim for is not so much a dualistic knowledge of facts—the possessor satisfied in the possession of useful information—as a unified sense of being *in* an experience, an involvement in *happening*. It could be said that poetry treats *being* as *knowledge*. This is often explained as an active passivity or potent acceptance or an oceanic sense of oneness with the world. This tendency in poetry, by definition, leads outside culture because it involves a capitulation to—a going over to—what we haven't made and can't control.

As Don McKay suggests in his poem "Sometimes a Voice (1)," there seems to be a nostalgia in words themselves, and in our voices, for their pre-linguistic roots—the way a domesticated animal might long to be wild again or a tool long to revert to the raw material it's made from—and poetry is one of the ways human knowing and language can get close to their roots. Poetry is language yearning not just to serve as a system of symbols for things but actually to be those things again, to join the things it masquerades as. This is what poetry tries to do: push language as far as possible into an enactment of the things it speaks of. It does this by using words not just for their denotations (their dictionary meanings) but for their layered associations and for their existence as physical matter, for their ear- and mouth-feel and mimetic ability. Poetry sculpts and dances with language and plays it like a musical instrument.

It is descended from the practice of casting spells, making time sacred and conjuring spirits. It has the power to introduce the poet and her listener or reader to heightened states of awareness. It draws on pre-linguistic modes of expression and communication common to the natural world: calls, gestures, images of smell, taste, and touch. Through shifts in tone, pace and style, a poem can signal what it's about to say before it says it, as though telepathically through a kind of pressure wave preceding the words themselves. An understanding is conveyed that is somehow essentially intuitive and silent: deeply human and broadly animal at the same time. In this way poetry brings wilderness indoors and leads us into the wider natural world.

This is paradoxical. Poetry is a quintessentially cultural practice; its use of language is the most refined, perhaps the most skilled possible, and yet it has a solvent effect on culture. It breaks down the familiar and alters our understanding. In this way its effect is similar to what we think of as wisdom, which involves regarding knowledge as making changes in (or acquiring adaptations in) the self—reconfiguring the self—in response to the world's resistance rather than reconfiguring the world to suit our wishes. Poetry changes the world not by physical force but by changing our understanding and awareness.

The wildernesses explored in poetry are varied. Don McKay and Gary Snyder write about outdoor wilderness, the actual land, and in Snyder's case, the possibility of living locally in harmony with it. Tomas Tranströmer and Emily Dickinson make us aware of an uncanny other dimension—the past, the future, the spirit world, some surrounding consciousness—shadowing our domestic lives like an aura. Rilke, a bit like Keats, experiences beyond culture a realm of eternal aesthetic transcendence. Paul Celan experiences wilderness as irremediable grief, which he tries to see as austere beauty but is unable to. The situation is similar for César Vallejo, although his grief and longing are very different, profusely passionate and surrealistic.

Another enlargement, perhaps, of the idea of wilderness is in the poetry of Matsuo Bashō, who in the last years of his life gave up his home and, like a wandering monk, devoted himself to travelling the countryside of Japan. In a sense he had renounced security for wilderness, but his wilderness is not of the kind we usually picture in twenty-first-century Canada, a landscape scarcely marked by humans; Bashō's wilderness is saturated with human history. Every mountain, headland, and offshore island recalls a traditional song, or a poem by a long-dead poet, or a legendary battle, or some event in the life of a legendary court lady or emperor. He toils along in rain and snow to visit tombs and ruined shrines where hermits once lived. In a sense he has not left his culture for nature; he has abandoned himself to his culture as a physical terrain constantly dissolving before his eyes.

His purpose in writing about the sights and experiences along the road is not to preserve them against the ravages of time but rather to record the ravages themselves, the inexplicable, dignified (sometimes comical) human experience of loving things, building them into a cherished community, and seeing them gradually washed away in the weather, seasons, and years. His wilderness is the action of time, the process of natural change whereby all things break down and merge and other things emerge. And paradoxically he captures his experience of this process on the page. He illustrates his culture's history subsiding into the natural world and his own life's journey following the same trajectory, but more rapidly and with his deliberate awareness and intent, all of which he reflects in his masterful art. So the page can dissolve both our culture's and our personality's enclosures and scatter their contents (memories, histories, narratives) across a landscape into · which they merge and beautifully, naturally sink.

And yet.

And yet, while the page can turn our attention to the great universe surrounding and pervading our culture and personal lives, while language can conjure a *taste* of wilderness, an ecstasy, a disorientation, a sense of oneness, is the page itself able to evoke in us a full equivalent to the *experience* of wilderness? Can we really get lost on the page? Can language act upon our emotions, our senses and intuitions—can it open us to discoveries and change us—the way physical experience can? Is the page as powerful and vast as the physical world?

I don't think so.

No words, however beautiful, terrifying, surprising, or disorienting, can serve as a substitute for the unmediated experience of the real world any more than the virtual reality of the computer monitor or TV can substitute for raw reality. Language shapes our experience of reality but can't replace it. We evolved in the natural world over millions of years. The energies and unconscious meaning we draw from being alive on the Earth are different from and more powerful than anything we get from an artificial symbolic system, however intimately our minds are aligned with it.

This seems to be the idea in the opening of Lao Tzu's *Tao Te Ching*: "The way that can be spoken of / Is not the constant way." We cannot capture the full reality of the natural world in words. This is also why so many spiritual practices recommend silent awareness without verbal intervention, even the practice of poetry.

Where I walked yesterday is now underneath. Snow fell in the night, loaded the trees' black boughs and turned the earth's page. In its dense whiteness the field is brighter than the baggy grey sky. Before I got up this morning, or at least before I raised the shade and sat down here by the window with my notebook as I usually do, a flock of wild turkeys crossed through the field. Their tracks blend into the snow's lustre as though no creatures have walked there yet or as if their marks fell with the snow.

How long have I been staring at this?

The deer I saw crossing through the snow yesterday are also underneath, inside the field. All the coyotes and wolves and foxes, all the animals that have crossed there this winter and last fall and all down through the years are inside the field. The fresh hay cut and baled and taken away on wagons, those events, those moments, are in there.

And what is inside the snowfield is not dead or even sleeping, it's changing, producing new things. It will become clover and tall grass again. It will be crisscrossed by animals and birds. I will be out there again in every weather and season. It will be different every day.

The snowfield is blank and potent, empty and full of potential.

People, especially as they get older, enjoy the reverie that comes with gazing at large open areas of the natural world that appear unmarked by humans or that have absorbed human markings: ocean, plains, deserts, forest panoramas, mountain ranges, snowfields, starry sky. The pleasure is complex, both chilling and comforting, nullifying and liberating.

Is there some relationship between these appealing unmarked regions and the unmarked page?

In Chekhov's "The Lady with the Little Dog," after Gurov and Anna have become lovers, they take a carriage out from Yalta before dawn to watch the sunrise over the sea. "In Oreanda [they] sat on a bench not far from the church, looked down on the sea, and were silent....The monotonous, dull noise of the sea, coming from below, spoke of the peace, the eternal sleep that awaits us. So it had sounded below when neither Yalta nor Oreanda were there, so it sounded now and would go on sounding with the same dull indifference when we are no longer here. And in this constancy, in this utter indifference to the life and death of each of us, there perhaps lies hidden the pledge of our eternal salvation, the unceasing movement of life on earth, of unceasing perfection."

The narrator presents this response to the seascape as a universal truth, an objective feature of the setting likely to influence anyone exposed to it. By presenting the scene in this way, we are given to understand that this powerful response to the sea reflects the thoughts and emotions that Gurov is experiencing, and it's also likely that Anna beside him on the bench is having similar thoughts. The sense that these thoughts are in the air, in the natural world, not just in Gurov's mind, makes it clear that he is encountering something larger than anything he has previously known, an enormous fact, a recognition that is now transforming him.

The dawn seascape is therefore both an exterior and interior vista, a kind of page through which a truth emerges and is clarified.

Gurov's life has changed, as he will later realize; he has fallen in love with Anna. He will need to begin living a dual life to maintain their secret relationship and to preserve the deepened, authentic life he experiences in her company.

It's not so much that the sea at Oreanda has illustrated or reminded Gurov of the brevity of human life or the falseness of the way he's been living but rather that, in experiencing the sea's message in Anna's company, Gurov is experiencing an inner self who is more authentic and honest, more alive to the world. He is brought into contact with his deeper self, his intuitive being, by thinking *through* or by means of nature. This is in fact how we always think most honestly—not as independent reasoners but as part of ongoing natural reality.

What I'm after here is an experience, not common, but known to many of us, in which subjective and objective experience merge, a wide-focussed state of awareness, let's say a kind of vacancy. What is perceived "in" nature in such moments is not strictly "other"; but something that embraces both awareness of our own "inner" thought and our perception of "external" phenomena.

All the benches looking out over water: reverie stations for reviewing life in the form of waves and clouds. A bench and a map table of water and sky on which to unroll the self. A place to sit and scan nature's great inclusive page, its forms and expressions hovering indistinctly just under the surface; but their broad meaning, their emotion, precedes them, and it's good to relax and take in their shapes and feelings in the water horizon or the snowfield without pulling them out as naked individual things you could say and repeat.

For the poet, especially, the page is often like this, a three-dimensional zone like a hologram that spans the border between inside and outside, between what's in back of the eyes and before them. It's a lighted clearing that creatures approach from out of the dark and withdraw from again. Its blankness is potent and active but often inscrutable and inclined to stay blank—notorious for causing anxiety. This might be the experience especially of young writers. Older ones, perhaps, are more apt to enjoy gazing out to sea or over a field of snow for long stretches, enjoying a sense of things happening inside, underneath, without wanting just yet to disturb the surface.

"Stage"

> p. 1: Götz Adriani, Paul Cézanne, and Walter Feilchenfeldt, *Cézanne Paintings*, trans. Russell Stockman, New York: Abrams 1995.

"We"

> p. 7: Michel de Montaigne, *The Complete Works*, trans. Donald Frame, New York: Knopf, 2003.
>
> pp. 7, 8: Lao Tzu, *Tao Te Ching*, trans. D.C. Lau, Baltimore: Penguin Books, 1963.

"Chart"

> p. 12: John Steffler, *The Grey Islands*, Toronto: McClelland & Stewart 1985; London, ON: Brick Books, 2000, 2015.

"Frame"

> p. 14: Daniel L. Everett, *How Language Began: The Story of Humanity's Greatest Invention*, New York: Liveright, 2017.

"Portal"

> p. 20: John Keats, *Selected Letters*, Oxford: Oxford University Press, 2009. See the letter to his brothers George and Tom, December 1817.

"Cutout"

> p. 22: Daniel L. Everett, *How Language Began: The Story of Humanity's Greatest Invention*, New York: Liveright, 2017.

"Half-Earth"

> p. 24: Edward O. Wilson, *Half-Earth: Our Planet's Fight for Life*, New York: Liveright, 2016. See especially pp. 8–9 and 185–187.
>
> p. 25: Henry David Thoreau, "Walking" in *Walden and Other Writings*, New York: Modern Library, 2000, p. 644.

"Dark Surface"
  p. 31: Knud Rasmussen, *Across Arctic America: Narrative of the Fifth Thule Expedition*, Fairbanks: University of Alaska Press, 1999.

"Battlefield"
  p. 43: Knud Rasmussen, *Across Arctic America: Narrative of the Fifth Thule Expedition*, Fairbanks: University of Alaska Press, 1999.

"From Behind the Page Something Pushes Against Each Written Word"
  p. 62: Robert Macfarlane, *Landmarks*, London: Hamish Hamilton, 2015.
  p. 62: Paul Evans, *Field Notes from the Edge: Journeys through Britain's Secret Wilderness*, London: Penguin Random House, 2015.
  p. 64: Margaret Atwood, *Selected Poems, 1966–1984*, Toronto: Oxford University Press, 1990. Reprinted with permission of the publisher.
  p. 66: Joseph Conrad, *The Nigger of the 'Narcissus'*, London: Dent, 1967.

"Aesclepion"
  p.93: C.G. Jung, "The Concept of the Collective Unconscious", in *The Archetypes and the Collective Unconscious*, Princeton: Princeton University Press, 1969.

"Colour-Thought"
  p. 100: *Chagall and Music*, ed. Ambre Gauthier and Meret Meyer, Montreal Museum of Fine Arts, 2016.

"Caution: Unstable Bridge"
  p. 101: Gaius Valerius Catullus, *The Poems of Catullus*, trans. Charles Martin, Baltimore: Johns Hopkins University Press, 1990.
  p. 101: William Carlos Williams, *Spring and All*, New York: New Directions Publishing Corp., 2011. Used with permission.

p. 104: The quotations from Herbert's "The Collar" and Donne's "Holy Sonnet 14" are from *Seventeenth-Century Prose and Poetry*, eds. Alexander M. Witherspoon and Frank J. Warnke, New York: Harcourt, Brace & World, 1963.

p. 105: Don McKay, *Another Gravity*, Toronto: McClelland & Stewart, 2000.

p. 106: Matsuo Bashō, *The Narrow Road to the Deep North, and Other Travel Sketches*, trans. Nobuyuki Yuasa, Harmondsworth: Penguin, 1968. Also, *Bashō's Haiku: Selected Poems of Matsuo Bashō*, trans. David Landis Barnhill, Albany: State University of New York Press, 2004.

p. 107: Lao Tzu, *Tao Te Ching*, trans. D.C. Lau, Baltimore: Penguin Books, 1963. See also the translation by David Hinton, Counterpoint, 2002.

"Snowfield"

p. 108: Anton Chekhov, *Stories*, trans. Richard Pevear and Larissa Volokhonsky, New York: Bantam Books, 2000.

ACKNOWLEDGEMENTS

In thinking of the page as a synecdoche or icon for all literature—especially for the practices of writing and reading—I have adopted an idea, an idiom, of Phil Hall's. While he was writer-in-residence at Queen's University in 2012, Phil inaugurated the annual Page Lecture series, which he named in honour of the Kingston writer Joanne Page and intended as occasions for writers to speak publicly about some aspect of their craft. Phil kindly invited me to give the 2016 Page Lecture. My talk, *Wilderness on the Page*, was subsequently published as a Fieldnotes Chapbook by Maureen Scott Harris and appeared also in 2017 as an article in the online journal *The Goose*. I thank Phil Hall for getting me started on this project and am grateful to Maureen Scott Harris at Fieldnotes and the editors of *The Goose*, Paul Huebener, Amanda Di Battista, and Lisa Szabo-Jones, for publishing early versions of this work.

Once I had begun thinking about the page, however—about writing and raw experience, language and nature, technology and wilderness—it wasn't easy to stop. My thoughts and questions went in various directions; there was more I wanted to say about writing, about my experience as a writer, than would fit into one Page Lecture. I began to merge essays and poetry, write poems in the form of essays, essays that thought like poems. I thank Jan Zwicky for engaging with the resulting manuscript so intricately, for questioning it and helping me to clarify and reshape it.

As always, I am deeply grateful to Susan Gillis for our ongoing conversation about poetry, nature, memory, and everything else. I thank her for sharing with me her imagination and love of language.

Some of the pieces in *Forty-One Pages* first appeared in *The Malahat Review*, *The Best Canadian Poetry in English 2013*, *The Best Canadian Poetry in English 2016*, and *Reliquiae*. A version of "Barrens Willow" is in my collection *Lookout*.

"The Day the Earth Smiled" is from a talk I gave at the *Speak to the Wild* conference in Wells Grey Park in 2013. I thank Trevor Goward, the conference host and organizer.

John Steffler is the author of six books of poetry, including *The Grey Islands*, *That Night We Were Ravenous*, and *Lookout*, which was shortlisted for the Griffin Prize. His novel *The Afterlife of George Cartwright* won the Smithbooks/Books in Canada First Novel Award and the Thomas Raddall Atlantic Fiction Award. From 2006 to 2009 he was Parliamentary Poet Laureate of Canada.

ᐅᓇᐃᐳ

OSKANA POETRY & POETICS

BOOK SERIES

Publishing new and established authors, Oskana Poetry
& Poetics offers both contemporary poetry at its best
and probing discussions of poetry's cultural role.

Jan Zwicky—*Series Editor*

Advisory Board

Roo Borson   Tim Lilburn
Robert Bringhurst   Randy Lundy
Laurie D. Graham   Daniel David Moses
Louise Bernice Halfe   Duane Niatum
              Gary Snyder

For more information about publishing in the series, please see:
www.uofrpress.ca/poetry

PREVIOUS BOOKS IN THE SERIES:

Measures of Astonishment: Poets on Poetry,
presented by the League of Canadian Poets (2016)

The Long Walk, by Jan Zwicky (2016)

Cloud Physics, by Karen Enns (2017)

the book of ayâs, by Neal McLeod (2017)

The House of Charlemagne, by Tim Lilburn (2018)

Blackbird Song, by Randy Lundy (2018)